This ...

paper? ...

Bears if he had any —
JUST RIGHT?

No other news, & ju...
love you.

Your boring frien

Nelle

Mockingbird Songs

Mockingbird Songs

My Friendship with

Harper Lee

WAYNE FLYNT

An Imprint of HarperCollins*Publishers*

"The Book of Camp Branch," poem reprinted by permission of Wendell Berry.

Letters used by permission of the Estate of Harper Lee.

HarperCollins books may be purchased for educational, business, or sales promotional use. For information, please email the Special Markets Department at SPsales@harpercollins.com.

FIRST EDITION

Designed by Leah Carlson-Stanisic

Library of Congress Cataloging-in-Publication Data
Names: Flynt, Wayne, author. | Lee, Harper, author.
Title: Mockingbird songs : Harper Lee : My Friendship with Harper Lee / Wayne Flynt.
Description: First edition. | New York, NY : HarperCollins Publishers, [2017]
Identifiers: LCCN 2016044095| ISBN 9780062660084 (hardcover : alk. paper) |
ISBN 9780062660091 (pb : alk. paper)
Subjects: LCSH: Lee, Harper. | Flynt, Wayne | Lee, Harper—Correspondence. | Flynt, Wayne—Correspondence. | Women Authors—Biography.
Classification: LCC PS3562.E353 Z63 2017 | DDC 813/.54 [B] --dc23 LC record available at https://lccn.loc.gov/2016044095

17 18 19 20 21   LSC   10 9 8 7 6 5 4 3 2 1

Contents

Preface xiii

Introduction 1

1   In the Beginning. 15

2   Celebrity, Kinship, and Calamity 27

3   Imperfect Fathers, Imperfect Towns 43

4   Contemporary Biography, Literary Disputes 67

5   Legacy and Change 85

6   An Author Shapes Her Own Identity 99

7   The Stroke and a Forced Return Home. 113

8   Marble Lady/Authentic Woman 137

9   Adulation and Isolation 155

10   To Everything a Season 173

Postscript 193

Appendix: Eulogy for Nelle Harper Lee 201

Acknowledgments. 211

To Alice, Louise, Nelle, and Dartie

Authentic Alabama Steel Magnolias

The song changes by singing
into a different song.
It sings by falling. The water
descending in its old groove
wears it new. The words descending
to the page render the possible
into the actual, by wear,
for better or worse, renew
the weary mind.

—WENDELL BERRY, "The Book of Camp Branch,"
from *Leavings: Poems*

Preface

———

On a crisp spring day in 1993 not long after I received Nelle Harper Lee's first letter, I was tending my rose garden when a male northern mockingbird began singing. Looking in its direction, I spied a calico cat halfway up a scrawny ten-foot-tall pine tree; up in the branches could be seen a small nest and chicks. The mockingbird, perched on the limb of an adjacent sweetgum, was singing fair warning of its intent to defend its family. The cat seemed frozen in space, torn between the nearby threat and the tasty morsels nearly within its grasp. Suddenly the bird dived for the head of the cat, which met the threat with an outstretched paw. The bird circled back to its perch and repeated the chorus of threats. When the cat resumed its climb, the bird swooped down again, this time attacking the cat's haunches. Now completely absorbed by the standoff, I put down my tools and watched.

After minutes of parry and thrust, advance and stalemate, the cat realized that the prize, however close, was not worth the risk to its life. But when the poor animal decided to reverse direction, it lost its footing. Frantically trying to regain traction, the cat part ran, part fell to the ground, an avalanche of bark bouncing off its head and back. The mockingbird, merciless, continued its attack as the cat tried to restore its breath and balance. When sufficiently recovered, the cat raced across my yard in search of sanctuary. The triumphant bird, apparently taking me for the cat's accomplice, swooped down at my head as I retreated into the carport. The mini drama concluded, the mockingbird returned to its perch in the sweetgum tree and resumed its singing.

Originally, the mockingbird's range extended toward Canada on both coasts of North America, but from the late 1800s to the early twentieth century the beauty and diversity of the birds' songs attracted not only mates but also trappers. So many were captured to be sold as pets that they became scarce at the upper edge of their range. After the so-called cage bird trade ended, the species recovered and pushed its boundaries north again. Although ornithologists inadequately understand mockingbird migration patterns, they have established that some birds move south in the fall, while others prefer the northern edges of their occupation zone.

Why Harper Lee named her masterpiece after these fascinating birds may be explained in one of its key passages. After Atticus Finch tells his daughter, "It's a sin to kill a mockingbird," Miss Maudie explains why: "They don't eat up people's gardens, they don't nest in corncribs, they don't do one thing but sing their hearts out for us. That's why it's a sin to kill a mockingbird."

Nelle Harper Lee was in many ways like the mockingbirds Miss Maudie described that hot Maycomb day. They are complicated and independent—and so was she. They boldly defend themselves and their families from predators, including the two-legged variety, and so did she. And like Nelle, mockingbirds have the most piercingly beautiful song. For that reason, she spent much of her life eluding people who wanted to capture and cage her. I loved and respected her for her fierceness and her commitment to singing the songs she wanted to sing the way she wanted to sing them.

Mockingbird Songs

Introduction

How does one chronicle a friendship? How does one remember the twists and turns, accidental meetings, serendipitous events, shared interests, and habits of the heart? How does a relationship progress from "Dear Mr. Flynt" / "Dear Ms. Lee" to "Dear Wayne" / "Dear Nelle" to "Beloved Professor" / "Dear Madam Famous Author" to "Dear Ones" / "Dear Prime Suspect"? How does mutual respect morph into formal acquaintance, warm friendship, and finally love?

These letters record the progress of my relationship with Nelle Harper Lee, but they can only hint at the reasons we became such special friends and correspondents, from the first letter between us, in 1992—when she was sixty-six and I was fifty-two—to the last, about a year before she died in 2016. Perhaps in another life Nelle wanted to be a historian of the South, as I have been throughout my career as a writer and professor. Or perhaps, as Nelle sometimes hinted humorously, she fell under the spell of my wife, Dartie (whose name confused Nelle for years as she tried to master my pronunciation), who brought her exotic chocolate concoctions and told her so many funny stories, and I was merely the appendage who came with the deal. Perhaps we became close because Dartie and I were there for her at three critical junctures of her life: when her sister, Louise, slipped into dementia; when she herself suffered a stroke and, obsessed with maintaining her privacy, isolated herself at a rehabilitation facility; and when she was forced to give up her second home in New York City and live out the rest of her days in Monroeville, the town from which she had fled to freedom sixty-five years earlier. Or perhaps we three met in the twilight of our lives and just needed each other.

Although Nelle and I communicated for more than twenty years, we never worked together, lived in the same town, or talked for hours on the telephone. Our friendship hinged on certain encounters, most of them face-to-face, and in between was lots of time and space—and letters. Her first to me was typewritten and formal. I didn't keep a copy of my response, but I remember that I replied in kind. She didn't write me again for a decade, not until a family crisis prompted her to reach out. From that point on, we both dropped our awkward formality in favor of ink-on-paper intimacy. Nelle preferred fine stationery. E-mail was never an option. Her letters were like those of two other southern literary icons of the time, Flannery O'Connor and Eudora Welty. Sally Fitzgerald, editor of O'Connor's correspondence, notes that the Georgia master of the short story had a reputation for reclusiveness "by inclination." But O'Connor, like Nelle, was also a witty and gregarious storyteller and conversationalist who often penned wonderful letters.

Though she lived into the age of personal computers, Facebook, and Twitter, Nelle rejected them, vociferously and profanely, believing them merely alternative ways of invading people's privacy.

Conversely, she once sent us a Charles Rennie Mackintosh card from her precious and dwindling stock purchased at the Hunterian Art Gallery at the University of Glasgow just because she wanted us to have one. Her letters are self-consciously of another age, less flirtatious, gossipy, and trivial than Jane Austen's, her literary idol, and more like O'Connor's and Welty's: colloquial, chatty, funny, satirical, brutally honest, unflinching, emotionally warm, intensely personal. Because her circle of close friends was small, her correspondence was doubly treasured. In time, others will no doubt share their hoard of letters to, from, and about Harper Lee, and an editor will compile them, as R. W. Chapman did for Jane Austen and Sally Fitzgerald did for Flannery O'Connor. This collection is, by comparison, small and far from comprehensive, but I hope it offers some interesting moments and important feelings in the life of my friend, and whets the reader's appetite for more.

As for the hinges to our relationship, these are easier to identify. We first met Louise—Nelle called her "Weezie"—Conner, and her little sister, "Doty" (a nickname of endearment for Nelle within the family), in March 1983 in Eufaula, Alabama. Louise—whose name Nelle would incorporate in her central character in *Mockingbird*, Jean Louise Finch (though the sisters would argue all their lives about who Scout really represented)—was the often overlooked second daughter of Frances and A. C. Lee. She had gone off to college at Auburn, fallen in love, married, moved to Eufaula on the banks of the Chattahoochee River, given birth to two sons, and become a mainstay of the First Baptist Church. Our paths crossed because she was serving on a committee to organize an Alabama history and heritage festival, and I, then a professor of history at Auburn University, about an hour away, was invited to be one of the speakers.

Decades earlier, during the civil rights movement, the mayor of Eufaula had asked Louise to serve on a much more important committee, one called Community on the Move. This five-person group had been started by a black woman Louise knew who was concerned about education, racial divisions, and drug trafficking in their town. Louise, asking the committee founder what she could contribute to the effort, was told simply, "You have a white face." Some local folks would have been offended by such tokenism. Louise agreed to serve. She and the other committee members met twice weekly, ate together, discussed community problems, and tried to make the town better. Her black friend began stopping by for coffee, a small act of personal friendship in most places but a racial blurring of the color line in civil rights–era Eufaula.

Citing her father as inspiration, Louise explained to us that he had been an "inside Christian," by which she meant a man of honor and personal decency, attuned to his duty as a community leader, one who treated all people fairly and with respect, though he was not liberal, self-righteous, or ostentatiously religious. His Methodist upbringing had persuaded him that the Kingdom of God was as much concerned with justice in Alabama as with heaven in the hereafter. Although he did not endorse the civil rights movement as early as Alice and Nelle, he moved more rapidly than most white Alabamians.

It was the history-and-heritage event that first brought me together with Nelle. Committee members wanted the keynote speaker to be Louise's famous sister, Harper Lee, but all were aware that she had made no formal public appearances in decades, except to accept honorary degrees. So they proposed instead to invite Nelle's childhood friend Truman Capote, by then world-famous for his book *In Cold Blood*. Hearing of this, Nelle stepped in. Knowing Capote's foibles and idiosyncrasies all too well, she feared that he would embarrass her sister, so she stunned the committee by volunteering to speak at the conference herself. It was an act of pure affection for her sister, but delivering on it was pure agony for Nelle, who had difficulty eating or sleeping for days before such an event.

Speaking just before Nelle that day was Nancy Anderson, a professor of English who was a colleague of mine at Auburn. Faced with both a large audience and a speaking slot that preceded a literary icon's, Nancy later told me she was feeling nervous and intimidated. But just before she walked onstage, she was introduced to

Nelle, who put her at ease by whispering, "Are you as terrified as I am? I feel like an owl that came out at midday. I let my sisters talk me into this, but I will never let them do it again."

Later on, Nelle talked for over an hour to a group of children who'd been in the audience, and offered to sign copies of *Mockingbird* for them. Among the fortunate recipients that evening was our son, Sean, who had turned fourteen that day. When I asked Miss Lee to sign our book as well, she replied icily, "I only sign for children." That was our first, not very promising, exchange.

A decade later, the Alabama and West Florida Methodist Women's Conference invited me to speak. At the reception afterward, two distinguished-looking women chatted with Dartie and me. Learning that one of them lived in Eufaula, I asked if she knew Louise Conner, whom I remembered from the heritage conference. "I am Louise Conner," she replied, grinning to assuage my obvious embarrassment. She then introduced us to the other woman, who was her older sister, Alice, well known to Dartie and me as one of the state's first female lawyers and a legendary leader of Alabama Methodism. Louise invited us to Eufaula for a visit, and we accepted, never thinking of Nelle or dreaming that she would mis-interpret our interest in her sister.

Louise was smart, warm, funny—and extremely fond of golf in general, and the British Open in par-ticular. During one visit, she delayed our departure for her favorite soul food restaurant so she could finish watching that tournament's final round. "Do you play golf, Wayne?" she asked, never taking her eyes from the television screen. "No," I answered. "Never liked it." "Well," she informed me, "you would like the open-ing event of the tournament. A Scottish bagpiper plays 'Amazing Grace.' When I die, I want a bagpiper to play that. I won't know whether I'm in heaven or at the Brit-ish Open, and it won't make any difference."

Soon we were visiting every few months, and our topics expanded to include our respective families. Lou-ise revealed that Nelle had warned her we might be less interested in Louise than in stealthily finding out about the Lees. In reply, I told Louise that we found her hospi-tality, wit, and wonderful storytelling much preferable to Nelle's abrupt dismissal of us years earlier at the auto-graphing. Louise paused, then replied, "Well, Nelle has to understand that Mother and Father were my parents too; and if I want to tell you about them, I will." And for years after that, she did.

During one of those years, a friend who taught literature at the University of Montevallo asked me to lecture an adult education class about poverty, class, and race in 1930s-era Alabama, which is the specific field of my expertise. Of course, that period is also the setting of *To Kill a Mockingbird*. I soon found that many of my students were lawyers and judges who were interested in studying the novel and its author. To my surprise, Alice Lee was among them, attracted, she told me later, by reading my accounts of life in twentieth-century Alabama. That seminar produced a long correspondence with Alice, fifteen years Nelle's senior, whom we saw infrequently but came to love.

Sadly, age gradually took a toll on Louise's health. First she fell and broke a hip. She recovered, but more falls forced her into an assisted living facility. Although we visited as regularly as before, she became increasingly distant, responding with silence to our attempts at conversation. One day her son Hank contacted us with the news he had moved his mother to a facility near his home in Gainesville, Florida.

Shortly thereafter, in fall 2002, the Alabama Humanities Foundation (AHF) honored Nelle with its highest award. She not only accepted but even agreed to attend the fund-raising reception. Although we had met her only once, years earlier at the autograph signing, we decided to attend in hopes of hearing news about Louise.

Our friend Nancy Anderson, serving then as an AHF board member, later told us a story characteristic of Nelle. She observed a mother, "not elegantly dressed like others," with daughter in tow, who had obviously spent more money than she could afford on tickets to the fund-raiser. The young girl carried a copy of *To Kill a Mockingbird,* despite a large sign warning "No Photos, No Autographs." Nelle noticed the girl, walked over to her, and asked if she wanted her book signed. When the excited child handed her the novel, Nelle saw that the mother had a camera. "You can take a photograph if you wish," she whispered.

Before the arrangements committee could whisk Nelle away to utter some variation of her standard acceptance speech (as I would come to learn, she'd usually just say, "I'm too overcome with emotion to say more"), I managed to whisper an inquiry. When the event ended, Nelle found me and pressed into my hand a program on which she had written her sister's Gainesville address and phone number. Delighted to have this information, we called Louise and wrote her, but received no answer; our friend had drifted away.

It was four years later that I next encountered Nelle. She had agreed to accept the Birmingham Pledge Foundation's Lifetime Achievement Award for advancing racial understanding, and the foundation's director asked me to speak briefly about her achievements. She was so well known that, although I am an experienced speaker, I struggled to write something that was not banal or trite. But in the end, something unfolded that night that was much more interesting than any speech I could have made.

I had spent the preceding months assisting two Birmingham teachers with a challenging project. Patsy Howze, a renowned choral teacher, had assembled a gifted choir at all-black Fairfield Preparatory High School, but the school had no theater where the singers could perform. Nearly all-white Mountain Brook High School, located in one of America's wealthiest suburbs on the other side of the city, had a state-of-the-art theater and Pat Yates, a gifted drama teacher, but only a handful of black students. And Yates needed more than that, because she wanted to do a production of *To Kill a Mockingbird*. She decided to propose a joint production with Fairfield, and asked me to join her and both groups of students to discuss it.

Our initial meeting took place at Fairfield, which none of the white students had ever visited. All the white students filed into the room and sat to my left. The black students gathered to my right. "What is the theme of the novel?" I asked the thirty or so teenagers. Silence. Prolonged, intimidating silence. I made a conscious decision to wait them out, but after several minutes I began to doubt my strategy. Finally, and to my enormous relief, a tall African American student with a deep bass voice broke the silence: "Tolerance! Don't judge somebody until you walk around in his shoes."

"Yes!" I nearly shouted. "And what does that mean to all of you and to this production?"

After that, we three teachers could not shut the students up. Work on the production began.

The night of the Birmingham Pledge Award, the foundation scheduled a reception for contributors who wanted to meet Harper Lee. She stood at the head of a long line that meandered across the lobby, greeting each person with a handshake and conversation, even though she was eighty and must have been exhausted. Just then I saw the joint high school cast of *Mockingbird* walk into the auditorium and get in line, each costumed and made up as the characters they were playing. (The foundation director had invited them.) Although many donors still needed to be greeted, I raced to the end of the line, corralled the kids, broke into the queue, loudly excused my rudeness, and told Nelle to sit down on the couch behind her because I had a surprise: the cast of the play I had told her about earlier in the evening had come to meet her. She sagged onto the cushions with an overly loud "Thank God!" and grinned as Atticus Finch, Scout, Boo Radley, Miss Maudie, Tom Robinson, Calpurnia, and all the rest posed for photographs and engaged her in animated conversation.

Within minutes the sponsors had escorted her to the front row of the auditorium and me to my chair onstage. That was the evening when Dartie, Nelle, and I began the process of transforming acquaintanceship into something much deeper.

1

In the Beginning

In an opinion column published by Alabama newspapers in July 1992, I paid tribute to the remarkable Lee family of Monroeville, especially Harper. In passing, I mentioned that I had read *To Kill a Mockingbird* in the fall of 1963, while I was in graduate school, only months after the terrorist bombing of Birmingham's Sixteenth Street Baptist Church. That murder of four young girls had so outraged me that, having left Alabama to study at Florida State University, I vowed never to return home to live. But after reading Nelle's novel—a luxury delayed for a few years by my doctoral studies—I began to reassess. It occurred to me that I knew many white people like Atticus Finch and Miss Maudie, as well as not a few blacks like Tom Robinson and Calpurnia. Nor was my state anything like H. L. Mencken's legendary "Sahara of the Bozart," a cultural wasteland. Alabama writers had claimed two Pulitzer Prizes for Fiction since

1933 (including one for *Mockingbird*, in 1961) and several National Book Awards, an impressive total for one of the poorest, least educated, and most backward states in America.

Louise Conner, who had become our friend by then, sent the column to Nelle. The letter she wrote to me about it, dated October 1992 but mislaid and not mailed until August, was our first written communication—but since I had left by that time for a semester of research and lecturing in China, it lay unopened in a huge stack of mail until I returned home early in 1993. Nelle's postscript, gently scolding me for referring to her as the oldest of the three Lee sisters when in fact she was the youngest (sixty-six at that time), set the tone for our later friendship: she was not one to excuse misstatements of fact, suffer fools gladly, silently dismiss literary misquotations, or allow anyone to invade her space without invitation. And if you did not want to know her candid opinion of anything, better not to ask.

 ·   ·   ·

When Alabama friends moved to Houston, Texas, in 1981, Nelle wrote the couple her impressions of their new town. The letter, headed "Dear Both"—which her friends showed to me years later and offered for inclusion in this book—captures the full dimensions of Nelle's sardonic wit, her dislike of the Lone Star State (San Antonio excepted), and her zeal for antiquarian bookstores and all things British.

○   ○   ○

The public image of Nelle as a private woman—opinionated, uncommunicative, cool if not cold insofar as human relationships were concerned—is far from the truth. She was in fact empathetic, warm, nonjudgmental, and a wonderful conversationalist, often going out of her way to answer letters to children, teachers, and fans, to attend award ceremonies for high schoolers who wrote essays about *Mockingbird*, to host friends visiting New York City, and to read and critique manuscripts by other writers.

No single letter better captures these qualities than one I received from a member of the audience at a speech I gave about Nelle in Fairhope, Alabama. In it, Mary Cameron ("Cammie") East Cowen described two encounters with the famous writer, thinking I might use them in a lecture I was scheduled to give at the University of Vienna. Cammie grew up in Mobile, where her parents

owned and operated a well-known antiquarian establishment, the Haunted Book Shop, which had sponsored one
of the first Alabama signings of *Mockingbird*. Based on
this casual meeting, Nelle later hosted Cammie, who was
passing through on her way to freshman year at Wellesley College, for a week in New York City.

∘   ∘   ∘

∘   ∘   ∘

433 East 82 Street
The Garden of Eden 10028

16 March 1981

My dear Both:
There are no chic people in Texas.

I spent some time in Houston a few years ago and found it to be the punishment for a mis-spent life, exactly my idea of what hell is like. No past, no future, just NOW in all its tastelessness. It's worse than Los Angeles, because L.A.'s hellishness has a certain dotty charm in places, an Oz-like quality of wish-fulfillment. Houston was destroyed and sown with salt in 1959. It was rebuilt all of a piece in the image of Jesse Jones and men of similar vision: The Galleria and River Oaks doubled and redoubled, containing Misses Ima & Ura Hogg. Your standard of living will be greater than anything you ever dreamed of, but just try to have a decent conversation with your air-conditioner. On the other hand, it might not be that bad: you are so far above the average Houston billionaire that in no time you'll be the cultural leaders of the town. Therefore, think not of what Houston can do for you, think of what you can do for Houston: teach them.

Venture out from Houston into the west Texas plains and you Alabama puritans will feel like old Roman voluptuaries. They are so clean-living out there they defy description. They are also rich.

San Antonio is the only town with any possibilities. It contains an old architect friend of mine whose wife lay down in front of bulldozers and thus preserved some of its character. They are rich.

Houston did have something once, but I got it: in a bookshop (the bookshop) I found to my astonishment four volumes of the old Strand Magazine, containing the original Sherlock Holmes stories, hot off the press! The fools sold the volumes for $4. In addition to not knowing the value of anything, they don't even know the price.

Come home, all is forgiven.

With much love,
NELLE

P.S. If you think of trying to play golf on that course in the middle of town, don't. A fifty-mile gale blows there at all times.

. . .

Harper Lee
433 East 82 Street
New York, N.Y. 10028

19 October 1992

Dear Mr. Flynt

 You do not let the semi-junk mail you receive pile up
to be disposed of every few months, as I do mine, so <u>you</u>
stay out of trouble.

 I was just going through the accumulation on my
desk: at the bottom I found three addressed, stamped
letters that I thought had gone out weeks ago. One of
them was a note to you, dated 3 August, and I shall
repeat what it said:

 My sister, Louise Conner, sent me a copy of your
article in <u>The Birmingham News</u> of 12 July.

 To learn that a man of your gifts, by faith in one
novel, chose to make his life in Alabama . . . makes its
author feel humble indeed.

I can only say thank you for honoring the state with your presence; thank you for your most kind article; thank you for the generosity which prompted it.

Sincerely yours,
NELLE HARPER LEE

That's what it said. It didn't say that in addition to the gratitude my family and I feel, you made Louise chortle with delight at one small error: actually, she's my senior by some years—I'm the younger. There was a brother between us who died at the age of thirty. His widow married again, and their children were brought up in Auburn.

That you are a noble man is the opinion of all the Lees; that you are a forgiving man is something I hope to discover if ever I have the pleasure of meeting you.

•   •   •

• • •

From: Cammie East
Sent: December 31, 1998 6:42 PM

Dear Dr. Flynt

Thank you for your talk in Fairhope a few Saturdays ago. I enjoyed hearing what you had to say, and you may even inspire me to get off my kazoo and send a note to Nelle and Miss Alice, both of whom I love dearly but with whom I seldom communicate.

I mentioned it to John Sledge, who was much interested in the possibilities for the book page, and indeed may have contacted you by now.

I can offer you one little tiny tidbit about Miss Lee that may or may not be helpful at your congress of Vienna; I don't think she'd mind my sharing it with you.

My father and Caldwell Delaney spotted the book right away as something remarkable, when it first came out, having read the pre-pub softback copy that Lippincott sent out (which is still one of my treasures). As I remember, they moved quickly and made arrangements to invite her to Mobile to speak at the library, and she agreed. Perhaps the library or its friends gave her an award—that part I cannot remember so clearly. I do remember that she began her talk in Bernheim Hall by announcing that she would first take off her shoes, which indeed she did, further scandalizing what I remember as some blue-haired ladies who weren't too happy about the book's racial themes to begin with. And that she was charming and dear, I thought.

After that session, she sent my parents a thank-you letter, in which she mentioned that she was working with some of the translators to produce international editions. I particularly remember that she mentioned that the Dutch one was having trouble understanding what a "spite fence" was, and that she was struggling to explain it. She also kindly and generously entertained me in New York for a week in September of 1963, when I was en route to Wellesley as a freshman and was foolish enough to believe that I had conquered the world. She put up with me nobly, put us both up at the Roosevelt and introduced me to the joys of 2 a.m. hamburgers ordered from room service, among other pleasures of the big city. I will always cherish the memory of her insistence that the two of us stand for hours on a New York sidewalk in a throng waiting for John F. Kennedy to ride by in his limousine as he went to speak at the United Nations. I kept insisting that she couldn't really want to wait there all that time, and she kept insisting that I should see the president. He was running late, but we waited, and now he's the only one I've ever seen in the flesh. And from what I've seen of most of the others, I think I'd just as soon keep it that way . . .

I will love her forever, even if I seldom communicate it.

Cammie East

o   o   o

2

Celebrity, Kinship, and Calamity

After our first exchange of letters in 1992–93, Nelle and I were out of touch for twelve years. During that time Dartie and I continued our friendship with Louise, only to lose her, in time, to illness and physical distance. After we saw Nelle at the Alabama Humanities Foundation awards ceremony, and she gave us Louise's address and phone number, I wrote her our thanks, and she replied, addressing me as "Wayne" instead of the earlier "Mr. Flynt."

The forthcoming movie she alludes to is *Capote*, staring Philip Seymour Hoffman in an Academy Award–winning performance as the narcissistic writer, with Catherine Keener portraying his longtime best friend, Nelle. Much of the movie focuses on the pair's journey to Holcomb, Kansas, to investigate the gruesome murder of a farm family by two drifters, and the writers' joint creation of a new genre of literature, "nonfiction

fiction" (for which Capote unfairly claimed sole credit). Before she ever saw the film, Nelle was told about alleged factual inaccuracies in it, and in her letter she expresses outrage over them. Eventually she did see the film, and liked it, especially Hoffman's portrayal of Capote. But she did find errors (for example, Capote is shown talking to one of the murderers in his cell, when in truth, Nelle says, they were allowed to speak to the prisoners only in the regular visiting area). Being herself, she wrote to the director, Richard Brooks, about his mistakes.

On September 16 I sent Nelle a copy of my newly published book *Alabama in the Twentieth Century*. In the last chapter, which details the accomplishments of Alabama writers, artists, and musicians, I had devoted a page to her.

The mutual friend whom I proposed we bring along on a visit was Kathryn Tucker Windham, a famous Alabama storyteller who lived in Selma and was a regular contributor to National Public Radio.

Nelle's February 18, 2005, description of Hurricane Ivan reflected both her rage at reporters who treated Monroeville's revered old courthouse as if it were more important than the town's people and her contempt for the state's political leaders, particularly State Supreme Court Chief Justice Roy Moore, who installed a huge granite copy of the Ten Commandments in the state's highest judicial building as a prop for his delusional gubernatorial and presidential ambitions. Her own health and that of her two beloved sisters was nearly as great a concern to her as storms and politics.

Her annual Christmas cards to us were unique reflections of her love for art and fine stationery, of New York City and Great Britain.

.   .   .

• • •

May 15, 2004

Dear Ms. Lee,

Thanks so much for Louise's address. I called twice, but she could never hear well enough to identify us. I have written as well, but I doubt that she will reply. Nonetheless, our quarterly visits to Eufaula to take your sister out to lunch, to watch the birds in her feeder, rock on the porch and swap stories constitute a memory bank from which we will make withdrawals for the rest of our lives. Louise is quite a woman.

Incidentally, the Lee legacy goes on in the Flynt family. Our son, who is a graduate of the Design and Art Center in Pasadena, CA, and now a designer/artist for Microsoft, and his wife (a brilliant young woman from the tiny coal town of Morris, AL) have wiped the sexist/racist dust of Alabama off their feet in their journey to a more liberal land in Seattle. But when they presented us with the first female offspring in three generations of Flynts, they named her Harper in your honor. I guess old places and people hold tenaciously onto us despite all our efforts to disengage. A piece of fine irony I believe.

Sincerely,
Wayne

°   °   °

2 August '04

NYC but soon home.

Dear Wayne:

Forgive me for not writing you—I've spent these
months in NYC going to eye doctors for them to
tell me they "can't do anything" and to Lighthouse
International to get magnifying glasses, electronic
Readers, etc. If you know anyone with macular
degeneration (the profession's euphemism—coined in
1962—for senile blindness) tell them the Lighthouse
shop has every gadget there is for the visually impaired
(Blind is now a no-no word, like sin). Will be home next
week.

[Louise's son] Hank Conner says that his mother
will not communicate by telephone. She has long since
stopped writing, and her sisters have given up trying to
reach her. She was so fond of you and your wife that I
hoped a call or letter from you would trigger a response.
You were two of her nearest & dearest, and if she will
not respond to you, I'm afraid we have lost her, that
nothing will bring her out of this awful thing she's in.

I am so greatly honored by my namesake. Your children have a chance to change her name before she learns it but I hope I won't give them reason to. Please convey to them my gratitude. They may indeed want to change it if what I've heard is correct: that a docu-drama will be made of Truman Capote's Kansas adventures and I'm to be in it. I'm told that the idea is that Truman fell in love with Perry Smith, one of the killers, & had an affair with him. No he didn't. I was there and the film-makers weren't.

Best ever,
NELLE

. . .

September 16, 2004

Dear Nelle,

We were distraught to learn your analysis of Louise's condition . . . The last time I visited her at the facility in Eufaula, there was some of the old, witty Louise; but she was also unusually reticent and withdrawn. We often had sat in the rocking chairs on her porch and watched the birds eat from her feeder. Sometimes we wouldn't talk, only watch and ponder. But soon she would be off again, discussing

the British Open or quizzing me about why people in
Alabama seemed so afraid of change. At the home, however,
the periods of silence increased until I finally felt like an
intruder even for being there . . . I know . . . what a special
and unique person she is, and we will always treasure
the days when we shared meals at her favorite soul food
restaurant in Lumpkin, Georgia, or the little Chinese
restaurant in Eufaula.

We were no less distressed to learn you have macular
degeneration. We do know people who suffer from it. In
fact, the man who taught Dartie and me ballroom dancing
suffers from the disease. Yet he is one of the finest dancers
I have ever seen and even travels alone to Rome to meet
his wife when she visits Europe on business. He has had it
ever since we have known him and manages quite well. I
suppose the disease affects people as Parkinson's does my
wife: horrible shock at the diagnosis, followed by depression
and anger, then by resignation, then by resolution and a
determination to live life as we all ought to live it anyway:
existentially. I love the Sermon on the Mount for people
like ourselves. We are given only assurance of this one day
anyway, so we rejoice in this existential moment. No one,
after all can count on more than that.

I hope you will accept this [book as a] small token
of the great esteem in which I hold you. I explain your

*relationship to the story in the preface and hope I do justice
to you in the final chapter (which by the way, is my favorite
chapter). There were so many people who have meant so
much to me . . . that I wanted Alabamians to know they
have much to take pride in beyond college football. I regret
that the book was so long, but . . . it took . . . awhile to
process half a century of observations about a place I care
about so deeply. . . . At least I hope my grandchildren,
Dallas and Harper, will grow up in Seattle with their
grandfather's perception of the people from whom they come
rather than the stereotypes of rednecks and ridge runners, of
Roy Moore and Fob James, of fundamentalist religion and
narrow-minded intolerance and gratuitous meanness. Since
you represent precisely what I want them to take pride in
(as do their parents), I am quite certain they knew exactly
what they were doing when they named her. . . .*

*I know this proposal may seem presumptuous, but if
you ever have a free day we would love to come down to
Monroeville and take you to dinner. We often take Kathryn
Windham out to dinner. . . . I know you two are friends,
so we would be pleased to bring her down with us if you
like. The advantage you have with us is I am no literary
critic. . . . I would, however, relish an evening of enlightened
conversation with a person whom Dartie and I so much
respect. And as I told Louise one time, I wasn't raised in a
family of huggers; though I am trying to do better in that*

area, for I have often regretted that I never hugged her and told her how much I loved her.

Sincerely,
Wayne

°   °   °

18 February '05

Dear Wayne:

By this time Harper Flynt (there is no more beautiful child) has entered the first grade and your whiskers have turned white. Before you fling this away w/contempt please let me say that I am deeply sorry for not having written and beg your forgiveness. If you can follow this cack-handed logic my silence has been a great compliment to you: I treat friends this way. Admittedly, they are thin on the ground now, but I don't write them until I feel I can give them my best. Poor as it may be, I still want to try, even if my best is a list of boring events.

To begin with, the date of your letter, 16 September, was a noteworthy one in our lives here. Ivan nearly devastated us. Monroeville did not get the publicity that Baldwin County, Atmore and Brewton got, but aside from the coastal destruction, Monroe County was one of the hardest hit. In Monroeville, 95% of the houses

were damaged (Alice is still waiting for a new roof); the
U.S. Engineers stayed here until well into this month,
supervising what seemed a perpetual cleanup job. No
lights for 10 days, no phones for 2 weeks in some parts
of town, no TV for over a month (a blessing) and erratic
water mains. All without injury or fatalities. It was
almost as if Someone didn't want to kill us but did want
to get our attention.

We spent the greater part of September 15–16 in
a bathroom at my nephew's house, Alice and I, Ed &
Marianne Lee plus their teenage daughter. The noise
appalling, the darkness visible, the radio stations off,
and not even cell phones working (they—the Lees—
live in a hole or something and couldn't call out. I don't
understand the things).

In my time I've been in two hurricanes: Ivan on land,
and Gloria, in mid-Atlantic. Monroeville was full of pine
trees, the Atlantic Ocean was treeless. The noise was
exactly the same. I guess it was the wind.

You did not read of Monroeville's plight because of
a star-struck young stringer for *The Mobile Register*.
A rinky-dink film crew was in town using the old
courthouse as a set for the trial scenes in their version
of the Scottsboro Case (complete with Redfordlike
young actor playing fat and bald Sam Liebowitz). Taking

no chances, the crew boarded up the windows of the courtroom to protect their investment. The total damage to the square was one fallen rotten oak (downtown was the least damaged). Young stringer reported only that the Historic Old Courthouse was saved, the *Register* & wire services picked it up and no further enquiries were made. Two weeks later I asked some *Register* friends, "What happened?" Their reply, "<u>What</u> happened?" (Hey Dr. Flynt: when does something like a building become Historic? There's not a blessed thing historic about the old Monroe County courthouse.)

Now from hurricanes we move to cataracts (one), heart catheterizations (one) ulcers (one), cholesterol (high), spread over the ensuing months to Christmas— all utterly time consuming and anxiety-making and adding to my disgust with the medical profession which is well on its way to becoming as contemptible as the legal profession.

Christmas and Louise. Wayne, the Louise we loved is lost to us. You were not the only friend who called and whose identity was not acknowledged. Hank says it's that way with friends and family; he doesn't know whether she truly can't identify people or whether it's an act—at any rate, the result is the same. He says that sometimes she fails to recognize people when she sees them. However, over Christmas she knew Alice and me and we had a most pleasant day together until poor Louise had an embarrassing personal accident and wanted to be taken back to the nursing home. She looks good—that good bone-structure keeps her forever fair of face to me. Hank says she spends her days sleeping and reading—he doesn't know how much she takes in, but she loves lurid true crime books. She will not walk except to meals. For someone who used to click off 4 miles a day, this is a profound change. She does not seek the company of others and stays in her room, another change. We could see an occasional flash of the old charisma, but it was only a small reminder of a most vivacious lady. I wonder if people will speak of us, Wayne, in the past tense before we die.

The latest is that Alice fell ten days ago and is still at home—at present in her lounge chair in the living room doing exercises ordained (or is it decreed?) by the hospital exercise person. Alice is truly and without a doubt the most remarkable person I ever knew. Totally deaf, with a cochlear implant, the surgery for which left her with no balance at all—a rag doll, yet—she manages to prevail over these handicaps with some sort of other-world serenity, going about her business—law business—as if she'd not a care. Until she falls. She seldom falls, but when she does she simply topples over;

until this last time she's not been injured. This time we fear a fracture somewhere because the pain is still as heavy as on the first day. She will make it, though, because she doesn't let this sort of thing stand in her way. (Only this time it's standing and she can hardly get up.)

So I've treated you to a Gilda Radner recitative ("It's always somep'n") of a semi-annus horribilis and don't even have a charred Windsor Castle to show for a string of clichés. (Which way does the accent go? I never knew.)

Now to important things: Harper Flynt is <u>correctly named</u>: she is beautiful, brilliant, feisty and without a doubt is a world charmer. She will go far in this world and bring honor and glory to her feeble old grandfather who just happens to be one of the best writers we have. When I say "we" I mean this USA. It is a great honor for me to be an extended member of the Flynt family and I mean that with all my heart.

I do so admire you. Not only your gift for making long ago and the more recent past come alive, but for the assured maturity of your style; here is a man, you think, who is fully grown—who has discarded, if he has ever had it—all bitterness and anger and writes about things with an unclouded clarity. I get so impatient with historians especially, who have an agenda, who can't just give us the facts without trying to persuade us of something. In the vastly dumbed down world, they don't seem to trust the reader to have the wherewithal to form an opinion. You do, and you flatter us while you make writing history the work of an artist. As was Macaulay. (Whig, my foot—the most clear-headed of his time.)

These days I must read with a magnifying glass and it takes forever for me to get through something: the one thing happy about this state of affairs is that my affliction has allowed me to savor the delights of Alabama In the 20th Century slowly, carefully, and with an almost palpable delight. It reads as through you had lived through it all. I can't wait for Alice to read it—she has waited patiently for all these months—because she has lived all but eleven years of the 20th century. She will agree with me that you told us who we are, where we've been and where we're going.

It looks like to hell if we don't get some things changed in this state. I dread the advent of Roy Moore's administration but it's coming sure as doomsday. What is wrong with us? Are you old enough to remember when people were less ignorant? I am.

I know another thing: you've grown older reading this.

With love,
NELLE

The Flynts rate one of my precious Chas. Rennie
Mackintosh cards: Nelle

* * *

William Glackens, "Central Park, Winter," 1905

Greetings of the Season: I've owed you a letter for the
past 5 years, it seems. If I live 5 more, you shall get one.
Much love to you and your wonderful family.

P.S. I have this great new light that almost writes for
me. Isn't my penmanship elegant?!

* * *

3

Imperfect Fathers, Imperfect Towns

Sharing news about ailments is not unusual among friends. It is probably even more common among the aging. Physical problems certainly help explain gaps in correspondence. Nelle's worsening macular degeneration would leave her nearly blind over time. But though limited vision restricted her reading, it neither sank her into depression nor tempered her opinions.

As a historian of all things concerning Alabama, and the author of ten books on the subject, I recognized early in our friendship that growing up in the house of her father, A. C. Lee—an influential state legislator who was once urged to run for governor—had stimulated Nelle's political instincts. So, too, had the family's strong Methodist ethics. Concerns about Klan-sponsored terrorism, the rise of the White Citizens' Councils (a sort of button-down-collar, better educated, less violent version of the

Klan), and the deafening silence of Alabama's white elites—economic, religious, and educational—left her as cynical about the state's politics as I was.

The Monroeville she rejected for Manhattan in 1949 smacked of suffocating insularity and parochialism. But after moving to her New York redoubt, she followed in the local newspapers as the situation worsened at home. She read of Alabama's massive resistance to integration. In subsequent years, White Citizens' Councils proliferated like kudzu. By 1957, when she stopped work on *Go Set a Watchman* and began enlarging a single story into *To Kill a Mockingbird*, her disillusionment with Monroeville had come to center on the town's racism and increasing violence against blacks. Still later, the state added nativism, xenophobia, homophobia, and a public school system that increasingly enrolled whites in private "Christian" academies while abandoning black children to increasingly underfunded public schools. More puzzling to Nelle than southern society in general was her own father's recalcitrance in the face of necessary change, and she wrote *Watchman* as a way of speaking for herself. In the novel, an adult Jean Louise Finch returns to Maycomb and is shocked to discover that her father and boyfriend are affiliated with the

White Citizens' Council. Turns out, Jean Louise's sense of justice and righteous indignation do not mix well with the complexities of family, community, and church in her hometown, and, reeling in confusion, she again forsakes Maycomb for New York.

In that way, Jean Louise parallels Nelle, who was reconciled in some ways to the imperfections of her father and her town but nonetheless found it impossible to live at home. Not until the publication of *Watchman* in July 2015, decades after her departure, would local citizens begin to understand the depth of her alienation. Although Alice and Nelle became more conservative politically with the passing years, until they preferred George W. Bush to Barack Obama, the sisters occupied the terrain reserved in Alabama for "progressives."

Nothing better demonstrated Nelle's lack of affection for her birthplace than her refusal to use her literary fame to promote the local economy, which faltered after the town's major employer, the women's lingerie company Vanity Fair Corporation, moved its manufacturing overseas. By the great recession of 2009–2011, the population of the county had declined by a third, and unemployment had soared to 23 percent. In response, Monroeville's Chamber of Commerce and educational leaders began to promote the town as "the literary capital of Alabama"—with good evidence. Tiny Monroeville boasted two Pulitzer Prize winners—Nelle in fiction and Cynthia Tucker, an African American who was then editor of the *Atlanta Journal-Constitution*'s editorial page, for editorial writing—plus Truman Capote and two twenty-first-century novelists, Mark Childress and Tom Franklin.

Although Nelle often noted the irony of the town's proclaiming itself a literary capital even though a local bookstore had closed for lack of patrons, Monroeville found ways to capitalize on its most famous literary resident. Every spring an amateur thespian troupe staged a sold-out production of *Mockingbird* in the old courthouse; the company even once performed the play in Israel. Piggybacking on that, the Alabama Writers' Forum began scheduling its highly regarded annual symposium in Monroeville during the theatrical season, attracting a star-studded cast of writers from across America.

One writer the symposium failed to attract was Nelle. She allowed her name to be used for the group's highest award, but she consistently refused to attend the event (in later years, she made one exception, to be described in future letters). As she writes, "I go to deep earth if I'm home when that thing's on." She once told Dartie and me that as soon as officials announced the date of the writers' festival, she booked a train compartment for California to visit the Pecks. In May 2005 that journey had special significance: the Los Angeles Public Library presented her its annual writer's award.

Nelle's busy May schedule did not prevent her from sending a beautiful miniature tea set to Harper Flynt in Seattle, where her grandmother Dartie taught her how to use it. Though Nelle's fictional ragamuffin, Scout Finch, relentlessly rejects her aunt Alexandra's efforts to turn her into a proper southern lady, our Harper took to the role like a duck to water.

In September 2005 I told Nelle that I had been invited to lecture at the Brooklyn Public Library about *Mockingbird*, the borough's scheduled "Big Read" for the following year, which would allow us to meet on Nelle's preferred turf. That month, the movie *Capote* was released, reigniting speculation about the many insinuations of the author of *In Cold Blood* that he had written *Mockingbird*. Nelle avoided all the reporters who wanted her to comment, but Melissa Block, cohost of National Public Radio's *All Things Considered*, tracked me down a few months later, on the morning of the 2006 Academy Awards, for an interview about Nelle and Truman. Luckily I was able to debunk the idea of Capote's secret authorship by quoting the great man himself. Jennings Carter, a childhood friend of both writers, had just donated a letter from Truman to the courthouse museum in Monroeville. Writing on his return from a 1959 sojourn in Italy, Capote said he had finally read *To Kill a Mockingbird* as it was being prepared for publication, and proclaimed Nelle to be a writer of exceptional talent. Gregory Peck's widow, Veronique, recorded the interview and played it for Nelle.

. . .

April 13, 2005

Dear Nelle,

I won't take offense at your delays if you won't take offense at mine. After savoring every word of your letter, I had wonderful intentions to reply promptly and thoroughly. Alas, it was not to be. And for some of the same reasons that cause your delay. Not long after receiving your letter, my beloved Dartie, a steel magnolia if ever there was one in these parts, grew weary of the worsening pain of five years vintage and consented to her orthopedist's recommendation of a complete hip replacement. . . .

After arduous physical therapy to prepare for the ordeal (complicated by her Parkinson's Disease . . .), she had the surgery on March 16. For two weeks she was in the hospital in surgical recovery, then rehab, returning home on March 29. Slowly but surely, she is regaining her strength, balance, and equilibrium; though patience has not been her strong point (nor mine for that matter).

I have always known that my career was made possible largely by her exertions, but I now have ample evidence of that hypothesis. I have washed and dried dozens of loads of clothes, shopped for groceries, cooked (at least under

*her careful scrutiny and with her detailed instruction),
vacuumed, cleaned toilets and baseboards, made up beds,
answered letters, written innumerable thank-you notes, and
generally conducted myself honorably if not always happily
or competently. This aging stuff is for the birds! And I will
be glad to get her back to normal, as the Muslims say "God
willing"!*

*Speaking of foreign religions, I often wonder if living
under the Taliban would be much different from living
under Roy Moore. Just trading one form of theocracy for
another, I reckon. . . . Although I am still Baptist (the
moderate Cooperative Baptist variety because the Southern
Baptists have gone [to quote the Bible] "whoring after
strange Gods"), I can't imagine a worse fate for America
than my brothers and sisters running the country. And
nothing gets my infirm Baptist deacon wife more riled than
the mere mention of Moore's name.*

*The news of your encounters with the medical
establishment, not to mention those of Alice and Louise,
resonate with our experiences. I do so hope that Alice is
better, though I think improvement for Louise is unlikely.
With three heart stents, I can identify with your heart
catheterization. That is not great fun, especially the hours
on your backside after surgery. . . .*

*. . . I will be in Monroeville for the writer's symposium
the first weekend in May. The organizers have a good lineup*

this year. . . . Let me know if you plan to be around and about during May 5–7, and I will take you and Ms. Alice out for some catfish if that is your pleasure. . . .

Miss Harper turned one yesterday. I am sending you a sample of photographs with identification on each so you can follow the progress of your namesake. She reminds me of one of James Agee's magnificent sentences in Let Us Now Praise Famous Men: with the birth of every child, all the possibilities of the human race are born again. This grandparent thing is a lot more spiritually satisfying than the Baptist church. . . .

Well there! I matched you page for page and with much inferior content. I guess that lays a bottom rail to our correspondence, so you can feel comfortable writing most anything that comes to mind.

Sincerely,
Wayne

• • •

○   ○   ○

30 April '05

NYC

Dear Wayne,

A quick letter to say <u>thanks</u> for a wonderful one Alice
forwarded to me here in New York, and to say that I'm
sorry I won't get to see you at the conference. (There was
no guarantee that I'd see you anyway—I go to deep earth
if I'm home when that thing's on, and so does Alice!)

I am on my way soon—anyway—for California
and won't be back in Alabama until about June or so.
<u>Then</u> I will try to do your great letter justice. Of course,
Harper's pictures are super!

In haste, with love,

Nelle

○   ○   ○

September 2, 2005

Dear Nelle,

*Well, I guess you have arrived at status beyond legend
or even myth. You have become a subject in what I once*

called a comic book but what is now called "a drawn novel."
Bert Hitchcock, a dear friend who headed the English
Department while I headed history (and who is a great
admirer of yours), brought this to me. His son, Eric, works
for Diamond Publishers, which is marketing the "book."
This copy is probably an advance copy, so I doubt it is
on the market yet. You can test your reality against the
author's mythology. I hope he understands Capote better
than [George] Plimpton and [Gerald] Clarke.

As you may have heard, N.Y.C. is reading To Kill A
Mockingbird during 2006, so I imagine those good folks
will hound you to death. The director of the Brooklyn
Public Library asked me to come up in May or June to talk
about you and the novel. I told him I would talk about
the Alabama context of the novel (Alabama in the 1930s)
and the impact of the novel both here and abroad (which
is mainly what historians talk about; and I hate literary
criticism as well as most people who read that stuff). So
I will be parking on your quarter in the "Big Apple" next
spring, which will give you a good excuse for spending some
time in Monroeville or some other remote, out-of-the-way
spot. . . .

Sincerely,
Wayne

∘　∘　∘

○ ○ ○

20 February '06

Dear Wayne:

Alice has turned her dining room into something
like the Texas Schoolbook Depository, and on the dining
table is a stack of manila envelopes containing mostly
books sent for jacket blurbs and letters—30 to sixty at
a clip—from miserable school children whose teachers
command them to write to me, then bundle up & mail
their efforts.

At Alice's command, prior to my departure from NY,
I have been going through them, and to my horror/
enormous pleasure, have discovered your wonderful
letter of last <u>September</u> and the not so wonderful comic
book.

Like Mr. Crocker-Harris in <u>The Browning Version</u>, I
AM SORRY.

Sorry that the Niagara of mail since <u>Capote</u> and that
<u>NY Times</u> piece has me floundering;

Sorry because sorry is what I am—sorry shiftless.

Please forgive me long enough to read that I am so
excited by the prospect of maybe seeing you this Spring
in NY. No, I'm the very last to hear of these things—
can't imagine sophisticated, cynical NYers reading

Mockingbird with more than amused unbelief. You are so right to enlighten these people with history that is not myth or TV movies. You will be terrific; you will bring to your audience(s) material unheard of by them and don't get me started on the prevalence of ignorance among people with access to instant information. That is one of the things you must explain when we meet.

From what I can make out of the comic book, where do these people get such strange ideas? I do laugh, though, because so much of Truman's own manipulative talent is being used on him—coming back to haunt him, as it were. I can hear him complaining, "Can they tell the TRUTH about it?"

No more than he could.

Wayne, if you haven't already memorized and burned these arcana, do so again:

433 East 82 St.

NY, NY 10028

(212) 744-2066

I have a cell phone but do not know how to answer it—just use it to call people.

Again, please forgive but don't forget me.

Love,

NELLE

∘   ∘   ∘

∘ ∘ ∘

March 6, 2006

Dear Nelle,

As much as it pains me to address you in your adoptive home of New York City rather than your <u>real</u> *home in Monroeville (even though I know it is excessively nosy and intrusive), I will send this through the mail in the hope that mail still passes from Alabama to New York. What with Roy Moore and his minions rampaging through the state, I am not sure any more what gets in and out.*

I am not altogether happy with Brooklyn right now. They just contacted me to announce that the "Read Brooklyn" focus of TKAM has been called off because the library did not receive a grant from the National Endowment for the Humanities. I called Mr. Kaplan and told him that I would come up for free (no grant needed!) if he would launch the program. He replied that, though grateful for the offer, he could not possible take advantage of me in such a shameless way. He plans to resubmit the grant next year, hopefully with better results. I still can't understand why you need a grant to launch a reading campaign for a book. My daughter-in-laws are so disappointed that I am contemplating coming to NYC anyway and treating

*them to the exoticism and excitement of the Big Apple. Are
you going to be around this Summer? . . . .*

    *Although I refuse to watch the Academy Awards
extravaganza, I was glad Hoffman won the best actor
competition. . . . Of course you will welcome a little respite
from the endless attention renewed by the film and news
of the July 1959 letter from Truman to his relatives that he
had read your manuscript and liked it very much. Melissa
Block, one of the hosts of NPR, called me last week to assure
the NPR listening world that his letter did indeed put to
rest the question of whether you did indeed write the novel.
Can you believe that? I told her that knowing Capote's ego
and capacity for manipulation, his failure (tragically and
unfairly, I believe) to win either the Pulitzer or National
Book Award, and his jealousy at the success of others, I had
no doubt that if he had written TKAM, he would certainly
have claimed credit for it.*

    *But at least the letter should end the debate. It came at
a wonderful time for me. Exercising my vast authority as
general editor of the new on-line Encyclopedia of Alabama,
I decided to write the entry on TKAM myself. I am going
to emphasize the contribution the novel made to one of
the most important issues of our times, the debate over
what democratic values public, private, and parochial
schools ought to teach. . . . Did I tell you that my son's*

*supervising teacher in Krems, Austria (where he taught
conversational English in an Austrian high school while
his wife completed a Fulbright year studying the Roman
Legion on the Danube) had him help teach TKAM as the
right-wing Austrian Freedom Party rose to power? In the
English language bookstore in Vienna, there were tall stacks
of TKAM in English, with a special discount price when
customers purchased 10 or more copies. How does it feel to
be the world's arbiter of democratic values?*

*One more item before I allow you to return to reading all
those letters from admiring Alabama school children. When
Alabama in the Twentieth Century first appeared, you wrote
me some extremely kind words about the book. Would you
extend me permission to quote that paragraph on the cover
of the paperback edition (if the press ever issues one; they
tell me the hard cover is still selling so briskly they have no
immediate plans for a soft cover edition)? If you have any
reservations about this just let me know. All the reviews have
been wonderful, and the press can easily find another source.*

*I hope you thrive in uninterrupted contentment back in
NYC until we are favored again by your presence.*

Sincerely,

Wayne

• • •

• • •

10 March '06

Dear Wayne:

1. By all means use any words of mine if they'll help
<u>Alabama in the Twentieth Century</u>. If you find them
insufficient, add a few of your own and put my name on
them. I love that book.

2. How much do you charge for all your services to
me? A California friend, Mirabile dictu, stored your
PBS interview in her magic machine and played it over
the telephone for me! Before I could write to thank you,
your great letter arrived. (It takes 4 days from Auburn
and 5 from Monroeville, for a letter to travel to New
York. For more reasons than one, I wish we could erase
Montgomery, through which <u>all</u> mail, it seems, must go.)
In his last years when every negative aspect of his
character—and there were many—ran out of control,
Truman <u>did</u>, I'm told, claim to have written most of
TKAM! This in a throw-away whisper to a bored (sorry
but in his cups he could be stultifyingly tiresome) band
of listeners. I don't know if you understood this about
him, but his compulsive lying was like this: if you said,
"Did you know JFK was shot?" He'd easily answer,

"Yes, I was driving the car he was riding in." I think that by the last years of his life, his miseries were so uncontrollable (word?) that he hated everything that crossed his path. He left a nasty little calling-card for all his friends, and Gerald Clarke made sure that, in his biography of Truman, they were delivered. Two come readily to mind: his odious claim that my mother tried to kill me (her reward for having loved him) and putting the words in Babe Paley's mouth about Slim Hayward: "Slim never really counted, did she?" Truman and his biographer shared some similarities of character: these were gratuitous shafts intended to hurt, and not necessary to Truman's biography. Oh well, it all comes down to one thing: I was his oldest friend and I did something Truman could not forgive: I wrote a novel that sold. (Never mind its content—I doubt that he ever understood what was in it.) Not only sold but was still selling in his last years. He nursed his envy for more than 20 years. Which brings me to

1. If TKAM can teach the Austrians democracy, then I'm afraid they might go to a Black-Belt Bourbon brand of it! No, I am so staggered by that news, I don't know what to say except to thank my translator. It's really incredible what is read into—or what people find in—

that story. I am most thankful that I'm still here with enough sense left to be thankful for what has happened with the years.

2. I'm with you on why it takes a grant to urge people to read a book; and to decline an offer of such importance as yours. It's no small thing: the living authority on all things Alabama (and Southern Modern), a speaker of such great gifts (you practice an art that's not dying but dead) offering services gratis—it's plain LOONY to cancel the project! Wayne, we live in weird times, and they are in Brooklyn.

3. Dear friend, if you & your daughters-in-law (or is it daughter-in-laws? You were in school longer than I) come to town, I deeply regret to say that you must frolic by yourselves. Alas, I'm now good only for lunch & dinner—no longer can I see what's on a stage or in an art museum or really hear anything. (One thing good: I no longer feel that I have to sit in church and listen to a preacher ½ my age.) That sort of thing is out for me now. But, for any meal—even breakfast, I'm your girl.

Maybe, though, by the time you get here, things could've changed: the eye-dr. here is leaning toward Avastin treatments for me. I'll find out Wednesday what goes, and what's involved. (Maybe they'll prohibit baseball, opera, ice skating, but I can't see any of that anyway.)*

Your verbose but deeply grateful,

NELLE

* When Henry V said old men forget, he forgot to include old ladies: I'm sure I've bent your eyeballs about the Mobile eye-drs. Nothing is what they wanted to do.

I don't know if the NY dr. can help me but at least he'll <u>try</u>.

If you are very good, Uncle Wiggly will tell you next time about a first experience for both of us (I <u>bet</u>): on my second visit to the 5th Ave. eye man, I was presented with a sweet-potato pie.

Now that's clout.

•   •   •

. . .

March 22, 2006

Dear Nelle,

  *How very much I enjoy your letters. Is it merely my
imagination or has email, with its 30 second mind bite,
completely destroyed the art of letter writing? Most letters
I receive electronically suffer from a bad case of diarrhea of
the intellect—chaotic bursts of something that is devoid of
all substance. I miss Shelby Foote, partly because he was
a crotchety old curmudgeon who could tell a story the way
it ought to be told, but largely because he wrote wonderful
letters and constructed his books with fountain pen on a
legal pad just like I do. Dear Eudora Welty also wrote grand
letters as did Flannery O'Conner (<u>The Habit of Being</u>
remains one of my favorite books). . . . And incidentally my
friend Suzanne Marrs at Millsaps College has at last done
justice to Miss Welty. Her new biography (<u>Eudora Welty: A
Biography</u>) sets the record straight. Ann Waldon's dreadful
biography was the Gerald Clarke version of Welty's life
(no one who knew Miss Welty would talk with her, so she
(Waldron) just used her fertile imagination to declare Welty
an ugly duckling and a Lesbian).*

  *I knew about Capote's subterranean campaign regarding
TKAM. George Plimpton interviewed Pearl Kazin Bell*

for <u>Truman Capote</u>. Bell parrots the typical anti–Harper Lee argument (if she had really authored TKAM then she would have written something else, etc., etc.). She told Plimpton that Capote "implied" that he wrote a "good part of" TKAM.

Melissa Block, the NPR reporter who interviewed me, . . . wants to do a much larger story. She kept asking me if we (you and I) had talked about the subject, if we were friends, etc. I told her we were acquaintances, had not talked about it, but I had my own theories. Based on Plimpton's interviews in Kansas with Clifford Hope and Harold Bye, and Truman's capacity to alienate everyone he encountered, I figured you had a larger role in the final completion of <u>In Cold Blood</u> that he did in TKAM. She allowed as how <u>that</u> would certainly create a firestorm. But I explained that the literary voices in Truman's book were no more your voices than the voices in TKAM were Truman's voices. But without your ability to calm the stormy Kansas waters, Truman would never have gotten many of those interviews. . . .

As I told Melissa Block, if Truman had written any part of TKAM, he would not have only hinted the allegations at cocktail parties, he would have flashed the news in neon on Times Square, especially in his hazy twilight years.

Incidentally, Louise was furious at the Clarke biography for claiming your mother tried to drown you and less charitable to Truman than you are. It was the only time I *saw her truly outraged. Needless to say, this is all private talk between us. Every time I lecture on TKAM, my wife, Dartie, makes me go over what I discovered on my own and can say compared to what Louise told me and which I cannot say. . . .*

I hope you received good news about your eyes. Any Yankee who can present a patient with sweet potato pie has to possess some rare insights. My wife, Dartie, has Parkinson's, so we know what the Bible means when it commands us to live existentially. This moment is mighty fine, and we rejoice in it.

As for our visit to New York, we are determined to come, book festival or not. . . . Our sons married two brilliant sisters (reckon keeping marriage in families is a southern thing?), and both can't wait to see the Big Apple. Of course, nothing would please us more than to take you to your favorite restaurant. Dartie has a hearing problem also, so I know how to talk loud to be heard. If the gathering takes place, it will be grand. If not, we will enjoy N.Y.C. vicariously for you. . . . By the way, one of my great regrets is my inability to arrange a meeting for you and Miss Welty while I was Eudora Welty Scholar at Millsaps College in 1992. She really admired your novel, was intrigued to learn more about you, and regretted that we were never able to bring that about. Too bad. You would have liked her. I only regret she did not have your good sense to tell people "no." She was so accessible that it caused her great physical discomfort and inconvenience. And that is something I never want to be to you.

There. I have written a longer letter than you did. You have my permission not to answer for a year or two, if you need it. I mainly wrote tonight to tell you that . . . little Harper Flynt turned <u>two</u> today. No doubt that little steel magnolia is already plotting how to get even with her parents by moving back to Alabama, living with her old granddad, and writing the sequel to TKAM.

Your friend and not acquaintance,

Wayne

o   o   o

4

Contemporary Biography, Literary Disputes

Talk of an upcoming biography of Nelle by journalist and former English teacher Charles Shields dominated Lee family correspondence and conversations for months before the publication date. Nelle, furious, complained of the numerous inaccuracies, but I was not entirely sympathetic, though I had not been one of his sources. Given how fiercely she protected her privacy, how the family had declined to cooperate, and how her friends, including me, had refused to talk with Shields, mistakes were inevitable. After the book's publication, in June 2006, I offered to interview Nelle for an oral history, which she could seal until after her death and deposit in the archives of her choice. I had taught a course in conducting oral history at various universities over four decades and knew that, under provisions of the 1973 copyright law, anything Nelle said would be entirely secure. I even volunteered in absentia the services of her two nephews, Ed and Hank Conner, who would have been better informed than I about family history. I explained that if she refused to talk with anyone about her life, Shields's narrative would become her biography, whether she liked it or not. But she was adamant: no living person should be the subject of a biography, and especially not her.

I was therefore highly skeptical years later when journalist Marja Mills claimed that during the same period in which Nelle was rejecting my proposals, she had begged Mills to write her "authorized biography." Nor was Mills's subsequent memoir, *The Mockingbird Next Door*, in any real sense a biography. It consisted of a few of Nelle's anecdotes that had delighted Dartie and me for years, some insightful family history recorded with Alice, and lots of information about Mills herself.

The Reverend Ray Whatley, who appears in Shields's book and comes in for criticism in one of Nelle's letters, briefly pastored Monroeville United Methodist Church. He apparently told Shields that Nelle's father had had him fired because his racial views were too liberal. Nelle always bristled at criticism of her father, but this claim particularly rankled. She often charged people she barely knew, as she does here, with trashing her parents, family, or friends for sake of their own fifteen minutes of fame. Nine years later, during controversy about the publication of *Go Set a Watchman*, she became angry at Mills and some Monroeville residents who claimed she suffered from dementia and was exploited by her attorney.

One friendship that did endure for Nelle was with Kathryn Tucker Windham. Both women were Methodists, attended the denominationally affiliated Huntingdon College, and became writers. Windham, who began her career as a police reporter in Montgomery during desegregation, became arguably the greatest professional storyteller of her time. Since by 2006 neither of them could drive, we sometimes picked up Kathryn at her home in Selma and brought her with us to Monroeville, where she and Nelle treated us to stories of their childhoods that kept us laughing for hours.

I sent Nelle a piece written by our son Sean about a controversial election in Austria. She obviously already had strong opinions about the country.

The "academy meeting" Nelle mentions in her July 12 letter refers to the annual induction ceremony of the

Alabama Academy of Honor (which claims to enroll the hundred citizens who render the greatest service and make the greatest contribution to the state) and to which I had been elected that year; the other new member Nelle mentions, Dr. Regina Benjamin, was a remarkable African American physician who then operated clinics for the poor in the fishing village of Bayou La Batre near Mobile. She was definitely not the prototypical member of the academy, which tended to favor rich, white, powerful, politically well connected males. Without Nelle's backing, Dr. Benjamin would have been at best a long shot candidate for election. In 2009 President Barack Obama appointed Dr. Benjamin surgeon general of the United States.

◦ ◦ ◦

Mockingbird Songs

· · ·

28 March '06

Dear Wayne:

Hurray!

1. Please let me know when you & dtrs-in-law (sounds Trollopian—or G & S!) will arrive. I think you've got my telephone #. I doubt if you'll need me to get any tickets, etc. because you can get them so much quicker without leaving your laptop.

2. You are the letter-writer, my friend. When better letters are written, you will write them.

3. I'm just now making this discovery and I can't believe it will last—my handwriting is returning to its former size! I'm still about 2 inches away from the page, am lying cater-cornered on the bed but I'm looking at the page sort of sideways instead of head-on. I <u>hope</u> this means something is happening from that first shot of AVASTIN!! I've just got up & roamed around the room (not far in this apt.), but the world looks the same as it always does. This may not last, but I'm thankful for anything I can get!

4. Now you might like to read the book of Job for a light-hearted contrast to what's coming, and if I'm going over the same territory, please forgive me—old, you know:

I am so glad the Flynts were friends with Louise, because it sounds like she gave you a fairly clear picture of our Mother and our home life.

The creep who has written my "biography" sent me the page proofs and a letter of thumb-your-nose blandness. His descriptions—indeed his information, I guess—of our family & life are bizarre to say the least, and our poor mother comes in for it again. Not that she tries to drown me, but that she stays in a sort of limbo of reality. Nothing could be further from the truth.

This is simply for openers. I haven't read it through— this miracle that seems to be happening with my 2-inch vision I don't think applies to everything—but what I have goes from fiction to nonsense. Firstly, and I guess my friends have held fast and remain silent, his source-material comes from (a) people with an axe to grind (Rev. Ray Whatley, who thinks my father got him fired because he was "liberal" at the wrong time. He may have been but what got him fired—and this doesn't seem to have occurred to him—was that he was a lousy pastor, totally unsuited for the ministry, who belonged at a desk—where he spent his career, serving his Lord

working with pension plans and doing a great job) to
(b) acquaintances from early childhood on, some of
whom I've never heard of, who seem to want their 15
minutes (Catherine Cobb, e.g., somebody who lived in
my dormitory at Huntingdon who was offended by my
bad language and lack of "finishing touches" never more
than an acquaintance, I guess needed to get in a book).

Indeed, it seems that—to paraphrase Mr. Carville
on the subject of Bill's lady friends—it seems that he
(Shields) went through the trailer parks of the internet
with a sign saying, "GET YOUR FIFTEEN MINUTES
HERE." The response was weird to say the least.

Now this is the most alarming thing in the book:
he has printed my NYC address down to apartment
number! The only reason I can assign to this is
pure spite, payback for my friends' non-cooperation.
Although the book is full of pages of errors—over two
pages e.g. of my Oxford experience, wrong year, wrong
everything that was some sort of canned account of an
exchange program—he took great care to describe my
neighborhood, building, and how to get there. Pure
spite, or so bush-league he doesn't know any better.

Now to matters different but no less unpleasant:

(I can't get over this—I'm SEEING IT!). Let me tell
you a small thing about the Ann Waldron Welty bio
(and this is for your eyes only—no point in stirring up

cold ashes). I've known Ann Waldron for some years.
Never a close [friend], but warm enough relationship to
meet once or twice per annum to celebrate the virtues
of a mutual friend, John Luskin (she was his favorite
pupil; I was just a friend) at the U of A[labama]. She
had done a biography of Hodding Carter (was horrified
when she discovered that he wasn't as liberal as she'd
thought) and Caroline Gordon (a fairly good piece of
work, I think) and was casting her net. She had hit upon
Welty. "But she's still living," I protested. "You can't."
I apprised her of my views on biographies of the living
to no avail. She would do it anyway. Since she was my
superior in such things—a career in journalism, widow
of an NY Times man, prolific output, and I a one-novel
wonder, I shut up. Upon meeting her again I inquired
how it was going. She let me know her primary sources
were almost non-existent. When it came out, I didn't
read it—I did not then & never will approve of full-scale
bios of the living. I think (and hope) the reviewers shot
her down, because she's been writing detective novels
ever since. It's been years since I've seen her; she lives
in Princeton. At any rate, I am so <u>thankful</u> that there's a
fine biography of Welty. She was my goddess, and with
Faulkner, I think are the TWO.

    Wayne, I'm sorry this has gone on so long, but
it's your fault. I don't know if it's the preacher in you

that inspires confession—I think it's because you are everything you are: vastly intelligent with a heart of equal dimensions, you are a rare man in this world.

Now that you've finished Job, try Lamentations.

Love,

NELLE

(More)

You deserve a break.

Kathryn Windham (whom I hope you know) can make a cadaver giggle, which she did me in a letter yesterday. It seems that she had heard from her old (87) friend Virginia McNeal. They were best friends at Huntingdon, and when commanded by their formidable English prof., Rhoda Ellison, to write a poem, Virginia's best (and immortal) effort was:

Dandelion, dandelion
Squatting on the ground;
If I were a dog
I'd like to be a hound.

To commemorate the event, every year Kathryn has sent Virginia the first dandelion from her lawn. Her thank-you note this year was something like "You are so famous and I'm not. I have only 2 claims to fame: I wrote a poem, and I was bitten by Harper Lee."

That announcement came at the end of a page. Meditation produced no memory of the event. Had I been in my cups?

Not this time: when the legislature was in session one summer, rather than commute on Alabama's red roads, Daddy & Mother & family spent it in Mtgy., where their friends the McNeals called upon them. Virginia, about 10, "looked after me" while the adults visited; apparently I sank my teeth in her arm, suddenly with no warning. I was 7 months old, but with enough teeth for her to remember it for a lifetime. This began my career of naked aggression.

. . .

• • •

April 17, 2006

Dear Nelle,

   Taxes paid! Nine day visit to Seattle for reunion with two-year-old Harper and five-year-old Dallas . . . over.

   Thanks for the wonderful insight to Waldron and the Welty work. I adore Suzanne Marrs, and though her biography of Welty is too dense and convoluted, it is brilliantly insightful and complete.

   As for biographies, I just finished Shields's biography of you on the return flight from Seattle. I learned lots of facts, many of them incorrect based on Louise's accounts. Worse, he understands almost nothing about Alabama and the context of the novel. At least Catherine Keener, who played you in "Capote," comes from a family of story-tellers in western Carolina, respects your privacy and tried to use that knowledge in her role (or at least that is what she just said a few minutes ago on NPR's "Fresh Air"). By contrast, I don't think Shields understands you or your family (indeed he makes Louise sound like she deserted the family and makes Alice sound like a Marine sergeant guarding the Lee guard post).

   But worst of all, his biography is pedestrian. There is no poetry to his writing. Not a single memorable phrase.

His prose does not soar. It sinks. As in the first inning of a baseball game, the count on your first biographer is strike three and he's out.

Have you ever thought of doing an oral history? Allen Nevins invented the sub-discipline at Columbia University in 1948 when he noted in N.Y. Times obituaries how many people who had lived enormously influential lives were dying without historic legacies. So he began interviewing them. The result is the largest oral history collection in the world at Columbia. . . . It is simple for the interviewee, who has to do no preparation, but hellaciously difficult for the interviewer, who has to research the entire life in order to ask the appropriate questions.

Best of all for you, the written transcript and tapes are governed by an iron-clad 1973 copyright law (since amended to make the rules even tighter) that treats both transcript and tape like a joint musical composition where one person writes the score and the other the lyric. Both interviewee and interviewer have to sign a formal legal document (which I circulated to Auburn University's attorney to make sure it was binding). Both can place any restriction on the transcript and tapes they request. For instance, I have sealed some of my interviews for the lifetime of the interviewer and interviewee (which is not uncommon). Archivists view the seals as absolute (indeed, when one Canadian archivist did not properly seal an oral

*history the plaintiff won a million dollar settlement; and
that is the only "mistake" of that kind I ever heard of).
There must be a number of people you know who could
conduct the interview, and I could send you one of the
legal forms. I know that Samford, Auburn, Huntingdon,
University of Alabama, the Alabama State Archives,
Columbia U., or any place with a professional archivist
and safe, secure archival storage, could care for the oral
history until you specify it could be used. That way you can
tell your own story in your own words and provide the core
element accurately to some future biographer who perhaps
has both a grasp for/of research and a capacity to write
prose worthy of your life. Even one of your nephews might
be a good candidate for the interviewer, and the archives
where they would locate it can provide the legal form. But
do not give transcript or tape to any archives without the
appropriate seals and legal forms.*

    *Perhaps I am old-fashioned about biography. But I still
believe a person should have the first option of telling her
own story.*

    *Dartie and I are off to Scotland and Ireland next week
with our best friends from Hong Kong days . . . we are going
to indulge in some superficial genealogy and some serious
vacationing. . . .*

                           Sincerely,

                           Wayne

Wayne Flynt

∘ ∘ ∘

24 June '06

Dear Nelle,

   We thought of you often in Scotland and Ireland.
Knowing as I do that you are as much historian as novelist,
I kept envisioning you at the Battle of Culloden or with Sir
Walter Scott in the Borders, creating Scotish nationalism
in the 19th Century from the historical fragments of Robert
Bruce and William Wallace. . . .

   Then, of course, in Ireland Yeats, Synge, Joyce, et al., are
omnipresent. As is the haunting, thrilling, amazing, life-
enhancing music.

   John McCracken, Edward Bunting, and other collectors
began recording in the late 1700s, and Co. Mayo became
for them and Ireland what Sumter Co. became to Ruby
Pickens Tartt, John and Alan Lomax, and to American folk
music. It was altogether an exquisite evening that we shall
never forget. . . . I wish you could have shared the moment
with us.

Sincerely,

Wayne

∘ ∘ ∘

○   ○   ○

July 7, 2006

Dear Nelle,

I meant to send you these two items by my son, Sean, when he was teaching conversational English in Krems, Austria. . . . Iorg Haider and the right-wing Freedom Party won control of the government, resulting in lots of American criticism of Haider and the Austrian people. Sean mobilized TKAM to implore Americans to adopt a more nuanced rejection of Haider without the typical American self-righteousness about a different culture. These are two of his efforts (the first in USA Today*, the second in* The Birmingham News*).*

Incidentally, I enjoyed your "Dear Oprah" letter [an article that appeared in Oprah Winfrey's O, the Oprah magazine*]. It took me back to Anniston in the early mid-1950s. My family were not readers, though my father did faithfully absorb the* Anniston Star *every day. But for books, I headed for the Carnegie Library with its spectacular collection of stuffed birds peering down from the top of shelves, as if some exotic Hitchcock movie had gotten out of hand and landed in Anniston. . . . I wonder how many first generation college students from my teenage years owe their*

love of reading to that Scottish émigré and philanthropic
capitalist, Carnegie?

● ● ●

12 July '06

My dear Wayne:

You are surely one of the era's foremost practitioners
of a moribund art; your letters, I hope, will be kept
forever, if not between hard covers, then on some sort
of celestial computer where they may be down-loaded
for all humanity to come. I read them in awe and with
gratitude.

Alice has your dissection of Mr. Shields's work and
won't let me have it back; I have your account of your
U.K. and Irish journeys and won't let her have it. Thank
you for that, especially, Wayne. It was like being there
again, which I won't be and your reactions & responses
to your experiences so vividly have preserved it for me.
You are a treasure.

I must say your children aren't very dumb. Sean's
account of his Austrian experience shows every bit of
his father's masterly use of words, and he exhibits a
similar clear-eyed vision of the world, which makes for

fascinating reading. <u>He can write</u>, Wayne. But I don't
have to tell you that.

For another reason, I'm so glad you sent Sean's
article—it dispels a "feeling" I've had about Austria
because of the following incident.

About 15 years ago, I was bidden by a friend to be
"nice" to a young (about 30 years old, note) Austrian,
of slightly upper-crust connections, and in town for
a month. I duly was, and in the course of a midtown
tour we stopped for a rest in Rockefeller Center where
Tass (nicknamed) remarked, "They have our flag there.
I didn't expect it." He pointed to the various national
flags around the skating rink. "Why not?" I asked.
"Because the Rockefellers are Jews." I said the last time
I checked, they were Baptists. "Oh no, Jews, just like the
others." The others were the people who kick-started the
U.S. like Andrew Carnegie, Collis P. Huntington, John
Jacob Astor, J. P. Morgan, et al? I asked: Even Henry
Clay Frick?? Yes, all Jews. Now this was an educated
young man. I didn't pursue the matter because I knew
it'd be futile to try to convince him otherwise. I felt sure
it was an example of an isolated case . . . "the Klan has
its points," but it gave me an irrational uneasy feeling
about his country. Had they not changed? Sean's piece
dispelled it, thank God.

Wayne Flynt

Do hope I can get to be with you & your gang at
the Academy Meeting! I may have to stick close to Dr.
Benjamin, whose nomination I seconded, but I will
fight my way through the crowd of your admirers to at
least say HEY! (I would have seconded your nomination
but you were already spoken for!)

Love,
NELLE

∘ ∘ ∘

5

Legacy and Change

As founding editor of the online *Encyclopedia of Alabama* (EOA), I commissioned several entries on Nelle and *Mockingbird*. For the author's biography I turned to Nancy Anderson, a professor of English at Auburn with a special interest in southern literature, whose knowledge of Nelle's career was as encyclopedic as the famous woman's privacy permitted. I reserved the article about *Mockingbird* for myself. Now I had finished writing the entry, and with fear and trembling, I sent a draft to Nelle for her critique.

Our correspondence also included her candid opinions about the club of good old white guys who had run the Alabama Academy of Honor from its beginning in the 1960s. When Tom Carruthers, a highly regarded partner in Alabama's most prestigious law firm, became its chairman in 1999, he opened the academy to the winds of change that were rippling through the state's political landscape. As each class of inductees more closely resembled Alabama's real population (including women such as Harper Lee and Kathryn Tucker Windham), they in turn elected an increasingly diverse membership. In August of 2006 I was asked to speak on behalf of the new class of inductees—an occasion that, more importantly, allowed me to introduce my children and grandchildren to Nelle.

During that same August, I lectured to ninety passengers aboard the iconic 1927 steamboat *Delta Queen*. I began my talk about Nelle by asking how many of the passengers—few of whom were from the South—had read *To Kill a Mockingbird*. Nearly all had. Then I asked how many had read James Joyce's *Ulysses*. Two or three raised their hands.

That fall, Nelle remained in Monroeville longer than usual to be honored by the Birmingham Pledge Foundation and to watch the casts from the Fairfield and Mountain Brook high schools perform their joint stage production of *Mockingbird*. James E. Rotch, who established the foundation, asked me to introduce her at the award presentation, which would be attended by several thousand of her admirers. The introduction, "Atticus' Vision of Ourselves," drew on the essay I had written for the EOA, Nelle's careful scrutiny and critique of it, my own reading of the Bible and theology, and my life-long involvement in social justice causes.

Nelle's letter describing her reaction to my intro-duction arrived weeks later, and revealed some of her thinking on a couple of topics that are important in un-derstanding her. The first was her lifelong affection for New York City and her voracious intellectual and liter-ary curiosity.

The other important topic is Nelle's religious belief. Despite her disdain for both my Baptist ministerial identity and institutional religion in general—which had so often disappointed her, despite the Lee family's fidelity to it and her own high regard for the works of British novelist and Christian apologist C. S. Lewis—she asked me to deliver the eulogy after her death. The eulogy, she specified, should be solely about her novel and the enduring moral values it conveyed. There was to be nothing about her personal or private life. So insistent was she on this point that she instructed me to send a copy of "Atticus' Vision" to Alice for safe-keeping and implementation. To be on the safe side of her heavenly displeasure, I also sent copies to Ed and Hank Conner, conveying her strict instructions to read it as I had written it, in the event I was deceased or unable to do so.

When Nelle alludes to the "greatest editor since Maxwell Perkins," she is comparing Perkins, the renowned Scribner's editor who worked with Thomas Wolfe, Ernest Hemingway, and F. Scott Fitzgerald, with the Christian saint and chief editor of the Flynt family— my wife, Dartie, who edited my drafts of "Atticus' Vision" and did not spare my feelings when critiquing my writing.

The last letter in this chapter is from Alice Lee, writing to thank us for a gift of roses, which we harvested from our seventy-seven bushes at the end of the long 2006 Alabama growing season. We gave them to Alice when we visited on December 2.

o   o   o

. . .

July 24, 2006

Dear Nelle,

We are all delighted that you plan to be in Montgomery on August 21. Dr. Regina Benjamin is such an inspiration: a woman who never forgets where she came from or the people who have been left behind. That the Academy of Honor is recognizing her is a sign of how far this state has come since the Academy began as a way of honoring conservative white males in the 1960s.

I am enclosing my essay on TKAM that will be included in the Encyclopedia of Alabama when it goes on line in December 2007. I tried hard to make sure I got the story correct, but if you find a glaring error, let me know. I hate writing encyclopedia entries: standardized form; turgid prose; everything truncated and over-simplified. But the last encyclopedia concerning Alabama (by Thomas McAdory and Marie Bankhead Owen) appeared in the early 1920s, so it is past time for an update. Just return the essay in the envelope when you finish reading it.

Since I was retiring, the folks at the Humanities Foundation insisted I was the only person who could call in enough I.O.U.'s to make the project work. We have

now raised more than one-and-a-half million dollars,
have a headquarters funded by Auburn, have recruited a
wonderful staff, have commissioned more than 500 articles
by scholars from around the world, and will launch our
venture next December. As "general editor," I exercised my
vast powers to preempt a few articles (the overview essay on
Alabama, the essay about poor whites, and TKAM). Bert
Hitchcock and Nancy Anderson (A.U. and A.U.M. English
profs.) authored the essay about you. . . .

After the EOA goes on-line electronically, I am sure the
University of Alabama Press will publish a print version of
the best material. Frankly, I care so little for electronically
derived information that I will rely on the printed medium.
But I know my way is not the wave of the future. It is
quite ironic that I, of all persons, who know so little about
computers and so dislike email, should be the general editor.
But at least I have recruited a remarkable group of people
who understand the technology. . . .

I predict TKAM will be one of the most frequently
referenced entries, so I want to be accurate.

Wayne

∘ ∘ ∘

. . .

31 July '06

Dear Wayne:

Your letters are never less than wonderful, a word I use sparingly, but not about anything you write.

What a project! It sounds absolutely first-rate in concept and will be, of course, with you doing most of it (as it appears to me). How lucky for the state of Alabama that you've retired: your retirement is like everybody else's full career, and to have you going at full speed makes us fortunate indeed.

Hooray!

I have noted some small things on the entry about me that I've penciled 1, 2, etc. on the manuscript but written out on an accompanying page. If some of the comments seem acerbic, they aren't meant to be. It's just old age, 46-year-old rumors, academic assumptions, & general crabbiness that provoked them.

I so look forward to meeting the Flynt tribe in Montgomery! It's the one thing I'm really excited about! (You'll soon learn that Alabama's 100 can be a boring lot, sometimes, especially ex-governors who get the floor and natter on about their achievements, or the world's most successful real estate mogul telling how he did it.)

I'm told that the present chairman, Tom
Carruthers, is the fellow responsible for bringing
some enlightenment to the Academy—i.e., suggesting
that women, scholars, & super citizens should be
included, to say nothing of writers and people in the
arts. Heretofore, with one exception (Nell Rankin, the
token EVERYTHING—female, artist, good citizen,
etc., elected in the 70's and alone until the 90's!) the
membership was composed by men who wished their
grandfathers had been Republicans. Tom has brought
the organization to its present deplorable condition: we
are taking in a poor black woman who works out of a
pick-up truck, and an old professor from <u>Auburn</u>, of
all places who has done nothing but write revisionist
history, and whom I would have nominated but Kathryn
Windham beat me to it.

Much love,
NELLE

1. I'm glad people love it in spite of these major
failings. I wonder what their reaction would have been
if TKAM had been complex, sour, unsentimental,
racially unpaternalistic because Atticus was a bastard.
TKAM would have received great critical acclaim (which
it did anyway) and not've had a second printing, but I'm
content with patronizing opinions & mere popularity.

2. " . . . story may have been based . . ." The story was not based on the Scottsboro case or the Walter Lett case. Because the two took place at the same time TKAM was set, this is an easy, "Harper Lee must have been thinking of . . ." sort of speculation so loved by academics.

3. TKAM was not formed by "a series of short stories." It grew out of one short story.

4. The novel sold 2 ½ million copies during its first year . . . is wildly wrong. I love the " . . . also won the Pulitzer Prize for 1961" afterthought!

5. I'm glad the public embraced TKAM in spite of the Modern Library list of the 100 greatest novels!

6. For "set in Monroeville, Alabama" read "small Alabama town." TKAM's popularity has caused Monroeville people to claim ownership down to the most insignificant character. "That was my Aunt Clara. She always said, 'Aw, shoot!' " was the most far-out attempt to be a part of the "in" crowd. Had TKAM sold 2,000 copies, I <u>could</u> go home again!

• • •

• • •

August 25, 2006

Dear Nelle,

   I can't tell you how grateful I am for your typical gracious attention to my family. They were all enchanted by the grand lady and still talk about the experience in a near mystical way. And as I observed your similar attention to so many others, I began to understand why you protect your privacy so firmly.

   I promised to send you a copy of my remarks, so here it is. I look forward to seeing you on the 13th in Birmingham. Jim Rotch has invited the casts performing TKAM at all-black Fairfield H.S. and all-white Mountain Brook to the ceremony, and they are ecstatic at the opportunity just to see you. Do Methodists declare sainthood? If so, you may be on the way.

Wayne

• • •

o o o

8 September '06

Dear Wayne:

Herewith another list of things to thank you for:

1. I've only just received the letter giving your account of the fortunate passengers on the Delta Queen—how I wish I had been among them! (The neighbor who forwards my mail to Monroeville elected to go to Italy for a month's vacation just as I came home & just as your letter arrived in NYC. The next mailing from her will contain threats to cut off things.) To wander along those waterways and be guided by Wayne Flynt is my idea of time spent in perfection—what a rich history, what a masterful interpreter of it! I sort of wish you hadn't told me of what I missed.

And I'm glad my nit-picking caused no offense—my bio is safe in your hands; ignore my carpings, just correct the errors—a few that are rusty with time. I trust you not to give me the resentments Mr. Shields assumed that I harbored!

2. Something I'd so been looking forward to, of course didn't happen, spending a few hours with you and

that wonderful family of yours. I got just enough of a tease to want <u>MORE</u>. I was gently handcuffed from the beginning, a beginning in the archives building that lasted until the academy meeting started and then . . . having to creep back to the seat where Debra Wilkins had put me—<u>not</u> with the Flynt family. If you think I was purposely avoiding you, please know that I didn't have a prayer.

The glimpse I did get told me that Harper Flynt is bright, feisty, a tomboy & rabble-rousing little girl who is satisfactory in every way and whose name delights me. And <u>beautiful</u>—unlike the other Harper. Her parents, grandmother & Uncle looked so attractively intelligent that I simply wanted to break loose and be with you, but of course, I couldn't. Promise me that somehow we can get together.

3. Kathryn Windham is being offered up to this year's Harvest Festival, crowned with fruits of the earth, for nominating you for membership to the Academy. The two people there who wondered why were given no doubt about "why" when they heard you. In the five years of new members' addresses, yours was far away the most impressive I've heard, and that includes Cathy Randall's house-grabber of three years ago. Wayne, you are magic. The academy is blessed by your presence.

With you in it, it truly means "Alabama's best." Slowly, I think we are going from B'ham real estate tycoons to include our best from all callings, and your election brings the endeavor to a new and successful happening: college presidents, yes—<u>history</u> professors, well, hey, this guy Flynt can actually speak our language! He understands that history <u>is</u> us—dollars & cents! He shows us that we can make more money if we're better citizens! Let's get us another professor!

The danger there, of course, is getting just any other professor. The one we have, we can't duplicate: superb intelligence and true charity are so rare, that only one professor in the South has this startling combination, and I'm lucky enough to be in his presence come Wednesday.

Love,

Nelle

I have a new light—yet one more! It's sort of blue, like the light T. J. Jackson gave off. Lets me write smaller.

•   •   •

∘ ∘ ∘

September 17, 2006

Dear Nelle,

Well you certainly provided an early Christmas for
50 teenagers from Fairfield and Mountain Brook High
Schools. For a woman renowned for her "aloofness" and
"shyness" you were mighty warm, kind, generous, and
social. So much for stereotypes! . . . . Knowing how excited
they were at the prospect of meeting you, I doubt any of
them slept much that night.

I am sorry the organizers kept you moving so frantically
all day, but at least you saw a side of Alabama that didn't
exist a quarter century ago: determination to face up to our
history, to claim it and profit from it. If our generation can't
rise to the challenge of change, perhaps those young people
and their generation can.

I can come down to Monroeville with Sean and Shannon
in November after Thanksgiving, or bring them down before
or after Christmas with their siblings from Seattle. We are
determined to have a short visit, to cause no commotion, and
to leave early. So tell me what fits your schedule best. . . .

I enclose a copy of my presentation from Wednesday
night [see page 17].

Sincerely,
Wayne

6

An Author Shapes Her
Own Identity

I experienced lots of deadlines, unrealistic expectations, and pressure in my career as teacher, historian, speaker, and writer. None, not one, even came close to the events of September 13, 2006. When Jim Rotch, founder of the Birmingham Pledge Foundation, asked me to present the tribute to Nelle at the ceremony honoring her lifetime of work on behalf of racial reconciliation, I accepted without thinking of the consequences: thousands of Nelle's adoring Alabama fans filling the auditorium; forty or so of the finest young thespians in the state expecting as much from my performance as from their own; only twenty minutes to render a life from the fragments of a single novel. The moment I stood up at the podium, I knew I should have said "No way." But I rushed on in. Given the deepening of our families' friendship in subsequent months, including a holiday visit to Alice's house in Monroeville and to the Lees' maternal Finchburg plantation home, it was a risk worth taking.

In her letter asking me to save the tribute to present as eulogy at her memorial service, she included an uncharacteristically romantic request to scatter her ashes above Manhattan if she died in the Big Apple. Although I never invaded her privacy by asking, I've always suspected that the desire she expresses in one letter, to die in the city and to have her ashes "scattered to the 4 winds of Manhattan," was inspired by the writer Damon Runyon's unusual funeral arrangements. When he died in 1946, three years before a literary, starstruck woman arrived in the city from Monroeville, Alabama, his body was cremated, and, according to his instructions, a DC-3 flown by World War I hero Eddie Rickenbacker (illegally) scattered his ashes in the sky above Manhattan. Nelle loved Manhattan and identified with Runyon, a journalist and short story writer who had fled his birthplace in the Little Apple (Manhattan, Kansas) for New York City. In his new home he celebrated the world Nelle also came to adore: Broadway; baseball; gambling; drinking; writing; living amidst America's most exciting literary culture; liberation from the restrictions of small town America.

One of those restrictions had to do with food. Whenever she got the chance to make fun of Monroeville's culinary offerings, she did; with typical hyperbole, she regularly warned us against expecting a decent meal; according to Nelle, the town had no satisfactory food on Mondays, or on Saturdays, or on Sundays—or pretty much any other day.

o   o   o

9/26/06

Dear Wayne:

Hang onto "Atticus's Vision of Ourselves" because I want you to read it at my memorial service, should I die in Monroeville. (If you aren't around, someone else will read it.) One hymn—The Lord's My Shepherd Crimond Tune [an older musical setting to the lyrics of a favorite traditional hymn]—and that's it. (If I die in NYC my ashes will, without ceremony, be scattered to the 4 winds of Manhattan).*

Because my bodyguard (will you believe it?!) whisked me away like I was Al Capone evading machine guns, I had no chance to tell you and the greatest editor since Maxwell Perkins that there is simply no way to thank you for the loving kindness, perception, generosity and genius of your latest gift to me, tendered in one of the finest speaking voices I ever heard and believe me, I was sitting close enough to hear you this time!

I did not realize that the B'ham News had contributed so much to the decline of print journalism—from the next day's account, you'd think that nothing really happened but the 2 schools' appearance. It was really upsetting that the awards ceremony was so ill-reported. They just plain missed the greatest presentation speech ever given for anybody and the audience's reaction to it. It sounded like Auburn had already stomped on Alabama this year. The lack of reportage made me wonder if a reporter was there.

One further note: sheer panic makes me charming & gracious. I'm so terrified by these things that I'll be anything I'm asked to be if I can just get through it without revealing the idiot behind the smile. Every time, I say it's the last—be it hon[orary] or other award—and every time it takes the better part of a week to get over the stage fright. (Nowadays I follow a mantra of great egotism: I'm older than anybody here, I know more than anybody here, so why should I be so afraid of anybody here? It works for about 15 minutes.)

How about after Thanksgiving for a visit? Our calendar looks clear of doctors' appointments from Nov. 28 (Tues.) through to Dec. 3, I think. Haven't

ckd. w/Alice's appointments; I suggest late Nov. or
early Dec. because things get bizarre around here the
closer Christmas gets—you may think us too old for
much, but somehow it's frantic before we are hauled to
Gainesville (23–29 this year) for Christmas.

May I warn you of something if Louise hasn't
already: Alice neither knows nor cares about keeping
house. (If somebody gives her a picture, she'll clap it on
a wall, or prop it up somewhere.) The only things she
cares about are a comfortable chair, a good reading light
and enough books & mags. She has these things. You
will shift for yourselves.

Thusly warned, I will tell you that we are so looking
forward to any Flynts who will make the arduous
journey to here! They will be received with great
warmth, though scant comfort. We will try to make
up for this with catfish, which is about all you can get
in Monroeville. (Don't come on a Monday or Saturday.
There is nothing to eat.)

Love to you both,

NELLE

*Forgive a pun: I'm deadly serious about this, and have
instructed Alice, who will surely outlive me, that these
are my wishes. You are the only preacher I want.

○   ○   ○

•   •   •

10/10/06

Dear Nelle,

I hope you aren't expecting me to deliver your eulogy anytime soon. Will I do it? Of course. How could I refuse you or Louise anything? And if Alice is as casual as you claim, we will love her just as well. We stand by the principle that an orderly house is the sign of a sloppy mind that has nothing better to do/know. Eudora Welty's house consisted of her, her cats, a few chairs, bottles of bourbon and scotch, and stacks of books. Why, I would even come to N.Y.C. to read "Atticus's Vision of Ourselves" were I certain the infidels would understand it (so your spirit could float happily in the winds over Manhattan and the Mets stadium [could this be the year of another world championship?]). And as for the <u>Birmingham News</u>, we are dealing with a paper that invariably endorses change one generation after it occurs. As long as you believe I got TKAM right, I could care less what anyone else thinks. For sure the audience understood my thesis and roared their approval of you and your book. . . .

I have included information about that eye procedure at University Hospital in Birmingham in case you did not see it.

Sincerely,

Wayne

. . .

11/11/06

Dear Wayne:

How about Saturday, 2 December for a visit from the Flynts? I think that's better than Dec. 3 because we'll have 2 chances for lunch instead of the one respectable place open on Sundays and of course is mobbed. You may not think so from my prompt reply to your last letter, but we are really looking forward to being with you, Dartie & any descendants you may bring along! Let us know if 2 Dec. is okay and I'll try to have the magazines & papers picked up in the living room.

The next morning, after the B'ham Pledge ceremony, I read the B'ham News account and wondered if any journalist had been present. It was all about me and the Mt. Brook-Fairfield school-kids whom I met at the endless reception. I was puzzled and not a bit annoyed that the News had relegated the Award ceremony to 2 sentences. Annoyance that turned to fury when, sometime later, Jim Rotch told me that the Editor refused to print your address without drastic revision. The man suffers from terminal pettiness, to say nothing of his ignorance. He just turned down one of the greatest essays ever written on a writer's motivations and intent in the creation of a work of fiction. Its analysis was as good as the novel!

I'm scared to write this, as things may be back [to usual] in Gainesville, but the news about Louise has given us a lift as has nothing in 2 years: her children say that she is responding to things and actually reading a little, seems now to remember things from 'way ago and—mirabile dictu has even laughed a couple of times. Once when told of the death (she didn't laugh at that) of Edna Rudisill, aka Tiny Faulk to us—a writer of several volumes of fiction shot with recipes—she learned that Ms. Rudisill left a final volume of Faulk Family Recipes. Weezie laughed. "Everybody knows the Faulks couldn't cook," she said, a remark we cherish because at the time it was made, her memory was right on target. So little can mean so much when there is a glimmer of light in her dark world. Keep your fingers crossed for her and remember she was for years a Baptist: your influence will be greatly appreciated.

Let us know if the 2nd suits the Flynts & what time of the day to expect them. We look forward

Love,

NELLE

°   °   °

•   •   •

11/15/06

Hey,

Just got your letter of 11/14. December 3 is swell with us if you are prepared to starve. A 1:30 arrival means everything in Monroeville will be eaten. No catfish on Sunday, and we are so small-town that the Meths. & Bapts. gobble in 2 shifts, after Early Church & Church, so food tends to run out by 12:30. Please come, but at your own peril. We are not prepared to offer you one crying morsel, but love you.

I wrote you suggesting 2 Dec. because the city would have 2 respectable choices, but since the Monroeville P.O. is like the Congo (last Monday no mail was put in P.O. boxes until the window closed at 4:30 P.M. because only one person came in that day! Can you believe it?) I doubt if you got it before your letter of the 14th.

Your letter indicates travels. I hope you are lecturing & charging enormous fees.

Love,
NELLE

•   •   •

•   •   •

11/21/06

Wayne!

Hooray for Saturday at 10:30 A.M. okay with you all? We are so relieved because Sundays in Monroeville haven't changed much from Sundays in Finchburg when you couldn't splash above a whisper, & laughter earned banishment. As I've indicated, in addition you will fast for the day, or share a late breakfast with Alice, which consists of a blood pressure pill, a glass of orange juice & one cheese straw.

The B'ham children would be horrified by us—not only wild untidiness—(you are too young to remember the Collier Bros.) but total indifference to décor.

In this house you will find one of the 2 genuinely modest human beings I've ever known. When I showed [her your] letter she said, "Shall I just fade into the background when they get here?" She truly did not realize that you are paying a visit to her more than to me, that you are already acquainted w/her through Louise, that this is a family visit, not a gawking session on either side.

She is acutely aware that communication is difficult, but is grateful to people who take the trouble to talk

Nelle dressed to the nines (a rare occasion for her) at the awards ceremony she attended at Montgomery's Davis Theater to honor the high school cast of the play. At this performance, attended by many state officials, she actually walked onstage to receive an award and congratulate the euphoric teenagers standing behind her. *Photo courtesy of Karen Doerr,* Montgomery Advertiser, *January 11, 2007*

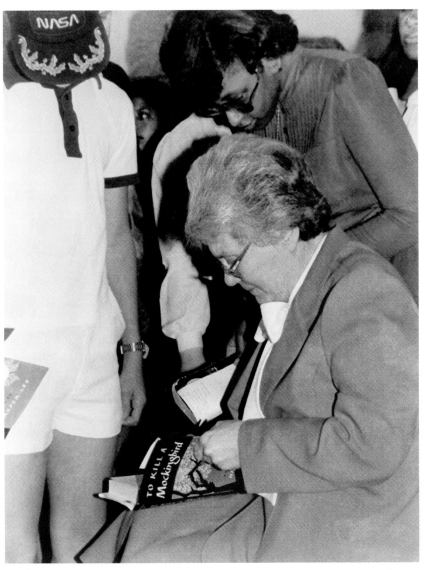

Nelle signing copy of *To Kill a Mockingbird* for Sean Flynt (wearing NASA cap) at Auburn History and Heritage Festival in Eufaula, Alabama, March, 1983. *Photo by Walter O'Neal*, Eufaula Tribune, *courtesy of Wanda Green, executive director, Monroeville County Museum*

Harper Flynt meets Harper Lee (looking a bit uneasy greeting her wiggly namesake) at the Alabama State Archives, August 21, 2006. Not pictured is a "boycott" sign advertising a display on the fiftieth anniversary of the Montgomery Bus Boycott, the background for Nelle's first novel, *Go Set a Watchman*, finished in 1956. *Photo courtesy of James Hansen*

Dartie and Wayne Flynt chatting with Nelle at a reception before the Montgomery production of *Mockingbird*, January 10, 2007. *Photo courtesy of Karen Doerr, Montgomery Advertiser, January 11, 2007*

Harper, Wayne, and Dartie Flynt chat with Nelle (wearing her "I plead the Fifth" shirt) at the Meadows Assisted Living in Monroeville.
Photo courtesy of David Flynt

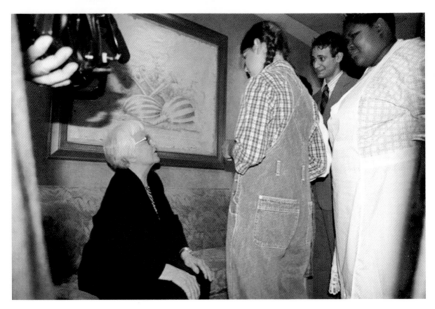

The cast of the Fairfield and Mountain Brook high school production of *To Kill a Mockingbird*, dressed as the characters they played, meeting Nelle at the Alys Stephens Center, University of Alabama in Birmingham, September 13, 2006.
Photo courtesy of Sandra Jaffee, producer of Our Mockingbird, *a documentary about the production*

Dartie and Nelle chatting in her apartment at the Meadows. *Photo courtesy of Lynn Barrett*

Alice as centerpiece on a fake hundred-dollar bill, an unusual pose for the precise and very particular woman. *Photo courtesy of Patrick and Tonja Carter and the Lee family*

Nelle, sloppily dressed as usual, with Wayne and Dartie Flynt, and Alice, elegantly dressed as usual. *Photo courtesy of Patrick and Tonja Carter and the Lee family*

Nelle selecting a pen from James E. Rotch (founder of the Birmingham Pledge Foundation) and his wife, Darlene, to use when signing the pledge. *Photo courtesy of James E. Rotch*

Collage of photos from Alice Lee's 100th birthday party. *Photo courtesy of Patrick and Tonja Carter and the Lee family*

Fairfield and Mountain Brook high school cast for their production of *To Kill a Mockingbird*, dressed as the characters they played, September 13, 2006. *Photo courtesy of Sandra Jaffee, producer of* Our Mockingbird, *a documentary about the production*

Wayne Flynt reading from Helen Simonson's novel, *Major Pettigrew's Last Stand*, as Nelle listens attentively. The bittersweet love story about a widowed Pakistani female refugee/convenience store owner and a retired British army officer and widower who had served in India, set in a provincial British small town much like Monroeville in its petty but loving ways, often reduced Nelle to either hilarious laughter or tears. *Photo courtesy of Dartie Flynt*

with her. Our friends do so cheerfully & they are rewarded. She's still brighter than all of us put together.

Well, you'll see us warts & all, and Julia's (who works for us) odd little fence she put up to protect one dim flower from Harry, the yard man who is simple & works for Alice because nobody else will hire him. (She is also noted for taking care of the blind, the lame & the halt—me, that is. She keeps me out of the Federal pen.) At any rate, come to see us!

Love to both of you,
Nelle

·   ·   ·

Law Offices of
BARNETT, BUGG, LEE & CARTER, LLC

December 11, 2006

Dr. and Mrs. J. Wayne Flynt
1224 Penny Lane
Auburn, AL 36830

Dear Dottie [sic] and Wayne:

As I changed the water to keep fresh the lovely pink roses from you, I was reminded of an incident in the life of my sister, Louise. Since you are the parents of two sons, it may bring a smile if you have not previously heard the story.

Louise had decided she wanted to grow roses. A bed was prepared in her yard and twelve healthy bushes were placed in it. Not long thereafter she came home and was startled to find that all dozen rose bushes had been very neatly removed. She questioned her younger son, then six years of age, and quickly got this answer: "I gave them to Benjy cause he had no roses at his house." Benjy was his black playmate who lives a short distance away. End of Louise's efforts in rose culture.

After your visit I faxed an account to Louise in care of her son, Hank. He read it to his mother to see if there would be a spark of recognition. No response. That gives you a report of the present condition.

Your visit is to be treasured and I hope that it will be repeated even though Nelle Harper should be in the City. I need an address for Sean and Shannon.

I look forward to receiving the Monroe County note. Perhaps you can bring them.

The huge tree cutting machine which was in the yard next to us when you were here finally took down the very tall oak which was leaning in the direction of the house and the very large limb that was spread over it.

The trunk was hollow so we breathed a sigh of relief when we look in that direction. The next Ivan or Katrina could have turned it to us instead of the direction it was pointing.

One more item: A neighbor brought us something for the meal last evening which was entirely new to Nelle and me. It was a grits pie! Have you ever eaten one? It's good.

Best wishes for a blessed Christmas.

Sincerely,

Alice

°   °   °

7

The Stroke and a Forced
Return Home

In January 2007 I suggested renewing our campaign to elect Alice to the Alabama Academy of Honor. Nelle, ever the shrewd tactician, investigated the number of deaths among members during the preceding year and concluded that we had little chance of success. Besides, her older sister had invested her life not in flashy leadership roles but in "serving humanity quietly, with modesty, with no thought of recognition or reward." Five years later, members of the academy would contradict our opinion of their values by sensibly electing the nation's oldest practicing attorney and one of the state's best people.

Alice's correspondence combined affection for Confederate ancestors and Alabama history with dislike of biographer Charles Shields and concerns about the worsening health of her sisters. In time, she added more personal regrets about her own loss of vision and hearing, particularly her inability to listen to sacred and classical music. Nonetheless, she stoically vowed to live for the future (even at age ninety-six) rather than retreat into memories.

In April 2007, shortly after returning to New York City from Monroeville, Nelle suffered a stroke and was taken to Mount Sinai Hospital. Partially paralyzed, she left New York by train several weeks later for the Lakeshore rehabilitation facility in Homewood, a Birmingham suburb. Homewood was less than two hours' drive from our house in Auburn, and so during this time our friendship with Nelle transitioned temporarily from correspondence to face-to-face visits. The small circle of people who knew about her partial paralysis was determined to keep the secret, and for years we did so. At first, we felt like snoops trying to infiltrate the Pentagon. There were false names, multiple personnel who screened us, and a near comical air of secrecy. After a while everyone learned who we were, which speeded up our visits.

The entire staff at Lakeshore was attentive to Nelle, and a welcome change from the technically proficient but cold professionalism she later said she'd experienced at Mount Sinai. We tried to help her cope with six boring months of physical therapy by bringing her a cassette player and our collection of books on tape. Her favorites were British comedian John Cleese reading C. S. Lewis's *Screwtape Letters* and Sissy Spacek reading *Mockingbird*, as well as Frank McCourt and Eudora Welty reading their own work—the memoir *Angela's Ashes* and the short story "Petrified Man," respectively.

As correspondence from Nelle declined, letters from Alice became more frequent. I commissioned her to write the EOA essay about Monroe County. Her declining health, too much knowledge of the subject, and an elderly woman's frantic efforts to care for her little sister prevented its completion.

When Nelle wrote at all over the next few years, her letters were brief. After nearly six months of rehab she moved to the Meadows of Monroeville, an assisted living facility in her hometown, reversing her flight to New York City and pretty much guaranteeing that she would end life where she'd begun it.

◦ ◦ ◦

•   •   •

Monday

Dear Wayne:

Alice & I were recently recalling the good things of the past year. You & Dottie were first on the list. You were so far ahead of everything else that everything else wasn't discussed.

After a night's meditation on the Academy project, Wayne, my feeling is no, not this year (But you will speak of the essense [sic] of time . . .), for these reasons:

1. She has outlived nearly all her contemporaries, those who knew her, and could testify to her remarkable achievements. Remember—and this hits me in some way every day—people younger than us/we <u>don't know what life was like before they were born</u>, and have little curiosity about it—

2. Alice does not have a Who's Who of being chair of this & president of that. She was awarded its first Citizen of the Year plaque by the Monroeville Kiwanis Club, though! She has spent her life serving humanity quietly, with modesty, with no thought of recognition or reward. (Example: she has educated more young people

than she can remember, asking to be an anonymous benefactor [and, her sister might have added, often funded by Nelle's royalties].) In short, she does not have a Pooh-Bah chestful of medals. She has never sought them. In the Academy, Pooh-Bahing helps.

3. Now we come to the real crunch: I think there are only 2 places available so far, and I haven't heard of serious illness in our group. Only 2 places, and our chairman is determined to fill one of them with the world's greatest living baseball player [Hank Aaron]. What our chairman wants he usually gets. (Always remember that!) I think our chances on that alone are very dim—one place and 35 nominees, probably—(Of course, a lot of B'ham lawyers & real estate moguls could be called to eternal rest this year, but I doubt it. They look exceedingly healthy.)

4. Although the shenanigans are supposed to be confidential, etc., and nominations are in secret, these things usually get out. I would hate it if Alice knew she was nominated but didn't make it. She'd be proud she was nominated: any ache she'd feel she'd keep to herself. I want to spare her that probability of disappointment.

Please let me know how you feel about this, Wayne; I've been in the Academy long enough to know a little of how it works, and I just don't think Alice could be elected this year. As far as I'm concerned, they should award her the whole state, but then she'd try to raise taxes [to fund decent schools].

May I call you this week? I'm sort of shy about phoning because your retirement is everybody else's full day.

Love to the Flynts
NELLE

o   o   o

February 6, 2007

Dear Alice,

I am writing a nomination for Leah Atkins for the Alabama Academy of Honor. When I finish it, I will send you a copy. We have so many remarkable women in this state that it makes no sense to have so few of them in the Academy. A few years ago, American historians were asked to list the ten most important women of the 20th century. Two of the ten— Helen Keller and Rosa Parks—were from Alabama.

In many ways you also blazed that trail through the wilderness. And I am glad that this past year brought us together. Louise has been such a dear friend that we are mighty glad to get to know her sisters as well.

Sincerely,
Wayne

.   .   .

February 6, 2007

Dear Nelle,

I hope you have found your return to N.Y.C. more restful than your stay in Alabama. I must confess that I did not fully understand why you spent so much time in the Big Apple until this year. The demands on your time are relentless. As you probably know, Huntsville is using TKAM as the city-wide reading program this year. The director of the library asked if I would help persuade you to come to the city this April. Shields and Badham [who played Scout in the movie] are going to speak. My job on the program is to explain Alabama in the 1930s as the setting of the novel. I explained to him that I don't get involved in your life, so he is contacting your agent. So be alert! Alabama will not let you rest! Like most things we love down here, we kill by holding on too tight and by demanding too much. . . .

Thanks for making this past year so special for the Flynts. When we once upon a time sat at Louise's back porch talking about you and your family, I often wondered if I would ever get to know you and Alice, whether "in the fullness of time" as the Bible poetically expresses it, our

*paths might cross. We are mighty glad they did. . . . we will
see you late spring or early summer in N.Y.C.*

Sincerely,

Wayne

°   °   °

January 22, 2007

Dear Wayne,

Please excuse my less than elegant writing paper. I
simply have to have lines. My writing tends to grow so
small that I can't read it, so I cross out and start again.

The carnations and mums on my desk are still very
fresh and continue to draw admiring comments from my
clients because of the outstanding color contrasts. I can
hardly wait for spring when my desk will have roses from
the Flynt Botanical Gardens.

The stopover by you and Dartie was a joy and I hope it
will be repeated many times. It doesn't matter that Nelle
Harper may be in NYC, we can still dine together.

I meant to inquire as to your planned route as you
continued south from Monroeville. Did you continue on
Highway 21 to the Atmore exit then on to I-65 to 59, or
did you leave 21 at Uriah and begin 59 through Stockton?
The latter route is more interesting. It basically follows

the Old Federal Road and those of us who follow it are convinced that when the paving was done no engineering was included in the project. The DOT [Department of Transportation] just paved over all the curves made by the covered wagons which zig zagged around impassable mud holes.

You may recall some years ago when a group of bored teenagers got drunk one Sunday afternoon and amused themselves by burning and vandalizing several black church buildings in the Little River community. Out of that episode came a small volume entitled "Ballad of Little River" which is not read for its contribution to the field of good literature, but it depicts quite accurately the route the kids travelled. The names of its roads, Mr. Peanut's store, are all there and you don't need a road map. The neat little white building you pass just before getting to Red Eagle's and Sehoy's graves is what arose from the ashes of the excitement of arson. Incidentally, those kids served prison terms of varying lengths. Makes me wonder about the outcome of the trial of more recent, older, better educated and more affluent pranksters.

Sorry you had to send NH a copy of <u>Poor but Proud</u>. There was a copy in one of the many book cases in this house. She did not ask me about it and of course her vision does not allow her to do much searching on her own. The hundred of books in this house would profit

from the labors of a good librarian who could bring them
into some order and let us know what we have. There
are two reprints that I always know where to find—
Pickett's History of Alabama and WC Oats History of
the 15th Alabama. Our father's copy is so worn that we
were thrilled to find a reprint several years ago. That was
the outfit of our poverty stricken grandfather Lee who
gallantly fought 4 years and who from Gettysburg took
the Bloody Road South and stacked arms at Appomattox
with the remnants of the Army of Northern Virginia.
Mr. Shields did not think much of him, but I would
like that gentleman (?) to know that I am proud to be
the granddaughter of that good man who came back
to the wasteland the Yanks had created and survived
Reconstruction.

While on the subject of Mr. Shields, I think he really
missed the boat when he did not delve a bit more in the
history of our First relatives and he could have done that
in his own backyard in Virginia. It would have been
much more interesting to his readers than such gems as
the number of manholes in N.Y. sewer system! Enough of
that character.

Honestly, I promised not to stay on my soap box.

Sincerely,

Alice

. . .

February 9, 2007

Dear Wayne,

Thank you for your note and the copy of your nomination of Leah Rawls Atkins for membership in Alabama's Academy of Honor. Nelle Harper is yet at home and she asked that I express to you her gratitude for the nomination. Of course there are 96 others who have to vote with you and N.H., but I cannot see how anyone could be less than impressed by the Atkins' record of service to education, sports, the business community and to the entire state.

I was impressed by the kindness of Sean and Shannon who sent me a lovely card from Florence. With the brevity of the trip and 24 college students to supervise, how could they possibly remember me and my mailing address?

This last year is memorable for me because it expanded our circle of friends to include you and Dottie and your children. I grieve that Louise cannot know about it and rejoice. Unfortunately, just hearing about it will not register nor be remembered by her. I am not one who wishes the past could be relived—I enjoyed most of it, but have always looked forward to things to come.

However, this is a situation to which I look back and enjoy the fond memory of some fascinating trips that the three sisters made together during the brief years between the death of our father and Hershel's myocardial infarction, after which Louise would rarely leave him overnight.

Several years ago, when I lost my hearing, music went out of my life, instrumental as well as vocal. The memory of sounds is still with me and when a good choir comes on TV, I turn off the sound completely and within the total quietness I "hear" those magnificent strains.

Nelle Harper is returning to L.A. next week. Don't be misled—it's neither Lower Alabama nor Los Angeles. It's to Large Apple.

Sincerely,
Alice

∘　∘　∘

April 16, 2007

Dear Nelle,

When Dartie and I returned from lecturing to the University of Sussex, Tom Carruthers called to tell me you were in the hospital. After the shock wore off, I have offered a great many prayers on your behalf (I am not sure God pays much attention to Baptist prayers anymore after we have made such fools of ourselves, but just in case God is as lenient with us as he was with the Hebrews, I will keep trying).

Enclosed are clippings with good news and bad news: bad news is that you lost out in the Birmingham idol cultural icon contest sponsored by (who else conducts such silliness) the Birmingham News: good news is that the BBC poll on world book day ranked TKAM 5th (behind Austen, JRR Tolkien, Charlotte Bronte, and J. K. Rowling) & one place ahead of the Bible. So you have now passed God but have not quite overtaken fried green tomatoes.

We love you and wish you a speedy recovery.

Wayne & Dartie Flynt

On the preferred writing paper for one with no balance.

●　　●　　●

• • •

April 27, 2007

Dear Wayne:

I am not sure just how much you know about Nelle's condition. The stroke paralyzed her left arm and left leg. Thankfully, she is mentally O.K. When friends found her, she was taken to Mt. Sinai Hospital and after about 10 days was removed to that part of the hospital which deals in rehab. She has now received the maximum of treatment and is waiting to be moved to Lakeshore in Birmingham. Paper work is underway for her acceptance there. In the meantime everyone is trying to plan a way to get her there. Nelle simply refuses to fly. She started back years ago when she worked for BOAC. She broke this rule on the occasion of Mother's death and that of our brother. She is determined to get to Birmingham by way of the handicapped room on the Crescent. I am told that she has limited movement in her arm and hand: that the leg in a brace allows her to "walk" with assistance. I put those quote marks for the reason that Nelle says she slides, while others call it walk.

The situation is simply horrible for me. To try to manage certain things that can only be done by me, and to have to get telephone messages through a third party is almost beyond frustration.

Things for me are really more distressing than you know. On March 1, our nephew's wife, Marianne Lee, unexpectedly underwent surgery for colon cancer. At the end of the operation, the surgeons thought they were able to get it all, but the pathology test said no. Colon Cancer Stage III, so she is now in the throes of chemo-radiation—chemo treatment which could be spread over a period of 9 months.

You have always heard that things happened in threes? The third was the unexpected resignation of my paralegal, without whom I am just lost. It was for good reason and she left with my blessing, but her replacement has a long way to go.

I am telling you all this to let you know that when I finally got around to doing my bit on Monroeville for the Encyclopedia of Alabama, I was really in no shape to do it, but I did try. I simply could not concentrate. My mind was always in N.Y. I know that I have embarrassed you with what I have done. It matters not to me if the committee just tosses it out and gets someone else to do it. It sounds like what it is: the rambling thoughts of a 95 year old woman who could not put her mind on what she was trying to do.

Will keep you posted on Nelle's whereabouts and her improvement. It will be slow, but she is determined to recover. Thanks to you and Dottie for your prayers.

My best to both of you,

Alice

•　•　•

April 29, 2007

Dear Alice,

Thanks so much for the update about Nelle. I suppose that news is the best we could have hoped for under the circumstances. Although I will be glad to have her close enough to visit, I fear that her anonymity won't last long in Birmingham, but perhaps I underestimate the professionalism of the staff at Lakeshore. Although the trip by train won't be pleasant, frankly travel by air is nearly as bad. There is a company in Birmingham, Medjet, that will fly her down, and the plane carries an entire medical crew. Of course, it is expensive unless one has Medjet insurance, which we have purchased during our overseas travel.

We were sorry to learn about Marianne's surgery. That is hard surgery, and I hope she has a successful chemo cycle of treatment.

As for your article in the EOA, don't fret. If you aren't satisfied with the article, just hold it until you feel better, or we can delay it. That is the grand byproduct of an electronic encyclopedia. If the article is not ready for publication when we go online late this year or early next year, we will just add it online later when it is ready.

Given the loss of your legal assistant, Nelle's problems, and all the other disruptions you have experienced, you don't need something else to worry about. You will certainly not embarrass or disappoint me in any way however it turns out.

Dartie and I are coming down for the Alabama Writer's Conference this weekend, and we were wondering if you might be able to have lunch with us Thursday. We plan to come by your office about 1:00 P.M. Thursday to see if you are free to eat lunch with us. But don't change any plans you have. We can be there at 12:00 if that fits your schedule better.

Sincerely,
Wayne

°   °   °

• • •

May 31, 2007

Dear Wayne:

My nephew, Dr. Edwin C. Lee, and I went to
Birmingham Saturday for our first visit with Nelle. We
found her looking amazingly well. It would be hard to
believe that she was so ill recently. The loss of 23 pounds
is a big plus.

She is quite satisfied with her new living arrangements
and already into the new patterns of her therapy. Her
telephone is right at her bed and if she is in her room will
answer it herself. This is her number:

1–205-868-2159

If you are in Birmingham in person and find
Lakeshore to visit, you will be carefully screened before
they take you to room 109B.

My best to you and Dottie,

Alice

• • •

° ° °

Monday

Dear Ones:

No sooner than your backs were turned, I put the
McCourt cassette on, only to discover a Welty disc in
the machine. She was reading the last line of "Petrified
Man," one of my favorites, of course. Please forgive me.
My holding a cassette from you is purely intentional.
You must ask me for it when next you visit, which I
hope will be tomorrow.

> I love you,
> NELLE

° ° °

22 August '07

My Both:

There is no end to your kindness—it won't even end
with you because you are forever. I guess that is not a
very learned or intelligent take on the hereafter, but
Wayne has read more on things eternal than I.

22 August

Would you believe I began this one week ago? I've
been companied out this past week. After therapies

there have been people every afternoon & evening. The weekend was guest-ridden except for Alice on Saturday who is never ridden although a guest.

Ed Bridges brought Kathryn Windham from Selma here. She was in full throttle and was hilarious. It seems to just come naturally. They are making strange whispers here—nobody will say anything except "when you get home . . ." etc. Oh well, it's always something.

Will you please thank the young ones for this delightful writing paper? It's like Baby Bear's if he had any—JUST RIGHT!

No other news. I just love you.

Your boring friend,

NELLE

o   o   o

∘ ∘ ∘

9/13/07

Dear Nelle,

(I hope you can read this with your new "eyes" [glasses])

How I miss seeing you as often as we did in August! We were too spoiled and cocky! Guess I must say I don't like the reality of having you there and us here in Auburn. We will be back in Birmingham for a few days with my ear surgery. That will be September 24th. We will see you then. We may pop in and surprise you. If the operation is successful, it will save time. We won't be saying everything twice as we do around here.

Now! As my wonderful mother would say "I have a bone to pick with you." How in all God's green world did you come up with the idea that you are boring??!! To quote our 6 year old: "THAT'S CRAZY!!!" If that is all you have to worry about, you must not live in the same world as the rest of us. You are bored with that place and all the hard work of rebuilding your body. But you are no more boring than Wayne Flynt or anybody I know.

However you came up with that idea, <u>FORGET IT!!!</u>

"End of sermon" (and end of my letter).

Much love and admiration

Dartie Flynt

○ ○ ○

18 October '07

Dear Ones:

They are springing me from here on 10 November, and I hope you can make it to see me before then if only to recover your property that you have so kindly left on what must be to you permanent loan.

I can't say a word about your generosity to me, because the ones I have are insufficient. None, not one, will do. So I will use two feeble words that are somewhere in the neighborhood:

THANK YOU.

The only thing that saddens me about leaving this place is knowing that I'll see less of you. You will, if you go down Hwy 21 from Mgy [Montgomery] find me on the right of the bypass: The Meadows assisted living establishment. If you come from Mtgy via I-65, etc., I'll be in the last white house on the left.

I love you

NELLE

○ ○ ○

. . .

October 20, 2007

Dear Nelle,

What wonderful news! If Lakeshore folks had kept you much longer, I was going to organize a posse of my cousins who worked for the Birmingham police force and we were going to storm that place and spring you.

We will come see you the first week of November, recover what you don't need (though we have one of those machines that plays CDs, tapes, and radio, so you keep that in order to remember us), and sit a spell. We will call before we come.

We will obtain further instructions about The Meadows at that time. And you may be assured we will find you wherever you hide.

I attended a Mary Reynolds Babcock Foundation meeting this week in North Carolina and talked with a board member whose friend in Atlanta had a stroke while in his 40s. He was in a coma and not expected to live. Now, five years later, his only symptom is a limp. So, sometimes progress can be slow but steady. It's like growing up when you are a child: it seems that every day lasts 24 hours but is much longer (that is a paraphrase not plagiarism, though I once read something like that in a novel about an undistinguished southern town).

We love you and pray for you every day.

Love,

Wayne & Dartie

•   •   •

8

Marble Lady/Authentic Woman

A key element of our friendship with Nelle was my refusal to treat her as a marble statue or unapproachable
titan of world literature. That was especially true after
her stroke and relocation to Monroeville led to a prolonged period of boredom. Knowing how much she rel-
ished satire, pretended insults, and witty rejoinders, I
did my best to spar with her. My letter of October 30 is
typical, although I turn serious at the end in express-
ing our pride at her receiving the Presidential Medal of
Freedom from President George W. Bush.

Nelle was determined not to receive the presidential award while sitting in a wheelchair. With courage worthy of Franklin D. Roosevelt, she attacked
physical therapy like a mockingbird pouncing on
a june bug. At the November 5, 2007, White House

ceremony, she was surrounded by Alabama congress-men who, given their records of racial intolerance, were most likely celebrating a novel they probably had not read and certainly did not understand. Vero-nique Peck was there, alongside Lee family members and lots of Alabama and New York friends. Nelle rose from her wheelchair, firmly grasped the arm of a tall US Marine, and walked slowly toward the president. Transferring her firm grip to the president's elbow, she listened intently as President Bush read the tribute to her.

When Nelle sent us a Christmas card with the printed message "Naughty or Nice: Which list are you on?" her response put me in my place and, as usual, won her the final word on the matter. In general, though, as Nelle's physical strength and sight declined, so did the content of her letters, which were more frequent but less consequential.

The "Society of Usual Suspects" mentioned in one of the letters was created by Nelle and resulted in equal parts from her literary imagination, feelings of bore-dom, and love for mystery novels and legal fiction. The dozen or so female members, Dartie among them, re-ceived a blue T-shirt bearing the society's name, a black

Mardi Gras mask, and a pewter pen. Nelle dubbed herself the Prime Suspect, and everyone involved had fun playing along.

On May 16, 2008, the Alabama Lawyers' Hall of Fame honored Nelle for combining legal education at the University of Alabama Law School, her father's noble character, and her imagination to create the fictional Atticus Finch, arguably the most recognizable and beloved attorney in the history of the English language.

The "Kathryn" I refer to is Kathryn Tucker Windham, who celebrated her ninetieth birthday with history's biggest ever wax-paper-and-plastic-comb band parade. (If you've never heard of such a thing, let me explain: You wrap a comb in wax paper, put your mouth on it, and sort of hum. The paper vibrates and makes a kind of music.) The event drew four hundred people, who took lawful possession of Selma's major thoroughfare in front of the public library. Kathryn led the throng of well-wishers in old-time Methodist hymns and congratulated God for providing a scorching June day whose noontime temperature of 90 degrees exactly equaled her age. When I related the story to Nelle on our next visit, she enjoyed it almost as much as the Chilton County peaches and Randle Farms blueberries we picked and brought to her.

Unfortunately, laughter died quickly at the Meadows, swallowed by the tedious monotony of life in assisted living. Letters from Nelle warned of fading short-term memory, although her long-term recollections were still sharp. In my nearly eight decades on earth, I have not encountered a professor of literature who had read so widely, remembered characters, plots, and settings so well, or was as capable of precisely quoting long passages from novels and poetry—and this at a time when her reclusiveness was feeding local rumors of senility or even dementia. The Nelle we knew and visited at least monthly was nothing like the one being discussed in Monroeville social circles, whose chatter reminded me of the conversations of the Methodist missionary society in *To Kill a Mockingbird*, or the hilarious gathering of empty-headed matrons at the tea party in *Go Set a Watchman*.

When my mother died, Nelle comforted me. As a Christian realist, she never attempted to portray life as easier than it was. Whether in her own life or mine, pain, tragedy, and suffering were exactly what they seemed. They could be borne, as she proved for the rest of her life, but never trivialized as "God's will" or seen as a burden too great to bear. Although her letter does not refer to C. S. Lewis's brilliant book *A Grief Observed*, she read Lewis voraciously, and her letter resonates with his wisdom.

○   ○   ○

∘ ∘ ∘

Wednesday

24 Oct.

Hey kids:

After calling the wrong no. & leaving 3 messages, Sara Ann Curry [the remarried widow of Nelle's beloved brother, air force major Edwin C. Lee] supplied me with (I hope) the correct one.

My message was that I will be away from here from · Sat. Nov. 3 to Tuesday Nov. 6. In Washington, yet.

I guess it'll be safe to confide in you that I'm getting the Medal of Freedom on the 5th. Stranger things have happened.

Sunday

Hey:

I've been trying to head you two off at the pass w/ phone calls (three of them wrong nos.) to tell you not to come the 1st wk of Nov. because I'm leaving for DCA Friday to be back Tuesday Nov. 6.

It's quite a journey for me, but I think worth it.

I LOVE YOU, NELLE

∘ ∘ ∘

• • •

Wednesday

1 November

Dear Ones:

Many thanks for your letter: This note before W-day is mainly to tell you (before I forget it so you can tell <u>me</u>) that my Monroeville (new) number will be: (251) 575-5673. It's unlisted, so hang onto this.

Will be back on 6 Nov., so please come if you can.

Much love,

NELLE

• • •

October 30, 2007

Dear Nelle,

Well I was disappointed in your media spokesman again. Here you go and win the Medal of Freedom and all you could manage in the <u>Birmingham News</u> was your picture on page 1; but the story was on page 3. You could not even eclipse Coach Propst and the Hoover High School football scandal, which earned star billing on page 1. Perhaps a

Nobel Prize for literature might eke out a narrow victory for front page space.

And does your trip to D.C. eclipse your trip to the President's box at Bryant Denny Stadium for the AL.– L.S.U. game? If so, how could you get your priorities so messed up?

I couldn't help but think of Mr. Faulkner's response to a friend at the University of Virginia when learning that the great man had declined an invitation to join other Nobel Prize winners and other literati at the Kennedy White House. Faulkner explained that Washington was just too far to travel for dinner.

Seriously, we are so proud of you we could burst! At last "W" gets one right. But even a blind squirrel can find an acorn once every six years. . . .

We love you!
Wayne and Dartie

* * *

10–29–07

Dear Wayne:

I see from the Ozark–Dale County Public Library flyer on the Big Read that you will preside at the closing ceremony on November 13. Your subject intrigues me.

Would it be possible for me to have a copy of your paper once it has been delivered? I would gladly reimburse you for any costs that might be incurred in reproducing it.

What think you of the last big shot on November 5 at the White House? That doesn't leave anything else to be had.

N.H. will ride the Crescent and Susan Doss will accompany her.

My best,
Alice

. . .

11/15/07

Dear Alice,

This seems to be my year for lectures about TKAM. I began with the "Big Read" in Huntsville in April. Then came Brooklyn Public Library, Columbus (GA), Enterprise–Ozark, Perry County in March, and Birmingham in April. . . .

I will record my lecture this time, transcribe it, and send you and Nelle a copy.

Dartie and I are delighted that she will be returning to Monroeville next week. I know there will be awkward moments, but I think she has made enough progress now to be fine. And she certainly wants to be near you.

It was such a joy to follow the events in Washington, especially her ability to stand. That is real progress. And what a wonderful tribute the President paid her, Gregory Peck, and your father. At last the President has done something with which I agree. . . .

Love,
Wayne and Dartie

＊　　＊　　＊

Nelle's Christmas card to the Flynts, 2007:

Naughty or Nice—
　Which list are you on?

This is not the card of my choice, but love anyway.

Nelle

＊　　＊　　＊

January 14, 2008

Dear Nelle,
　This letter is designed to fill you with guilt; that, of course, is what Baptists are famous for. But my strategy is even more sinister. Since you already feel badly that you

have not written us (something we never expected from you anyway), I thought I might as well give you a <u>real reason</u> for feeling guilty instead of a false one. For during the time you have been in Monroeville, I have sent you only <u>one</u> piece of correspondence and even that was a two or three sentence Christmas card.

Now there, don't you feel better! Now you have a basis for your guilt, which is so much more spiritually satisfying.

Seriously, we know writing letters is a chore for you. Nor do we measure friendship by the quality or quantity of correspondence (though you are one heck of a fine letter writer). Besides, we will see you soon in the flesh, as the apostle John would say.

Meanwhile, here is the newspaper clipping I mentioned to you about your obscure book. And here also is the schedule of Jane Austen films on APT.

Sincerely,

Wayne

· · ·

• • •

Monroeville, AL

5 March '08

My dear Ones:

   At my request they took down the THURSDAY
sign from the bulletin board & replaced it with
WEDNESDAY, much to their embarrassment. Truly, I
was beginning to get upset when you walked in. I knew
you hadn't come yesterday.

   Such is this hive of activity that the current day of the
week is a note worthy event and it takes this long to tell
you about it.

   I TREASURE EVERY MOMENT of your visit. Present
tense because it will stay with me for a long time.

                                                    NHL

• • •

9 April '08

[To Dartie]

   You are a founding member of the Society of Usual
Suspects with all the privileges accruing thereto. There
are no rules, no officers, no fees. You may call a meeting
by saying the immortal lines from <u>Casablanca</u> . . . .

"Round up the usual suspects."

This will cause your conferees to emerge from
their various lurking-places. Your membership badge
accompanies this.

HARPER LEE
PRIME SUSPECT

o   o   o

Dear Prime Suspect (AKA NHL):

*I am greatly honored to be among the founding members
of the Society of Usual Suspects. It is exactly the kind
of privileged group I wish to belong to. (Perhaps it will
redeem me from the audacity of resigning from the Auburn
Women's Club without having to die to be removed from its
roll.)*

*My first action as a privileged member is to call a
meeting with the Prime Suspect for lunch on Thursday,
the thirty-first of April at 11:00ish in the morning. I will be
the one in the hat and membership badge. (I will bring a
close friend [Wayne Flynt] who will not be wearing a hat
or badge.) We will confirm all this with you by telephone. I
look forward to our visit.*

Dartie Flynt

o   o   o

●   ●   ●

May 27, 2008

Dear Nelle,

   Well you certainly were a garrulous "famous person"
10 days ago in Montgomery. Instead of "You have left me
speechless. Thank you!," you actually poured out 13 words
by my count: "Thank you." Long pause. "I think that I will
hang out my shingle this afternoon." If you don't be careful,
pundits, critics, journalists and "Nelle-watchers" in general
will stop referring to you as "silent Nelle."

   I was pleased that the presider mentioned the "usual
suspects" so they can all receive the attention they deserve.
At first, I was unsure why you created this secretive cabal.
But after last Friday I believe I have solved the puzzle: any
attention deflected on them is less directed at you. What a
devious devil you are!

   Seriously, it was a great day, and we appreciate your
allowing us to participate. This Sunday we plan to drive
over to Selma to make sure Kathryn receives all the
attention that 90 years on this planet entitles her to. . . .

   I hope that all goes well with you and that your therapy
is progressing nicely. We will see you soon in Monroeville.

Love,

Wayne

∘ ∘ ∘

11 July '08

My dear Both:

For the peaches, blueberries & cake <u>I thank you</u>; but for your benign & saintly selves I thank you most of all! You are two of the treasures of my life and I love you,

NELLE

P.S. August? It can't come soon enough!

∘ ∘ ∘

July 21, 2008

Dear Nelle,

You remind us of a mature romance: it may come late but it is nonetheless rejuvenating and welcome. Every time we come to Monroeville, we return with three hours of conversation about you, Alice, and all the Lees. I assure you that you have enriched our lives more than we have enriched yours. Just watching you and Dartie laugh with such gusto and talk with such conspiratorial glee is one of the highpoints of my life.

We now have my mother moved to assisted living, her house sold, and our lives as normal as they are likely to be.

She has adjusted well and seems relieved to no longer have
to drive, cook, or clean.

See you soon.

Wayne

•   •   •

30 (or 31—I'm bats—July)

Dear Wayne:

The only thing I have to report is that Tom
Carruthers said he couldn't recall the word
"ineluctable," which I used to describe the passing
of days here. He said he hadn't heard it in so long he
couldn't remember it.

Well, the days <u>do</u> go by with ineluctable sameness,
but I feel most fortunate that they go by for me at all,
lorn lone creature that I am. I probably wrote you all
this before, but then I seem to have written everything
else before—what? Before God & the doctors decreed
that I should lose most of my marbles as well as most of
my short-term memory.

I can remember Mrs. Gummily though, and marvel
at the creative power of her Creator. I guess Dickens was
our greatest novelist although I don't like to admit it—
Thackeray was just as good in his own way . . .

There go I, like John a 'Dreamer'—lone & forlorn with everything against me.

If you hate my handwriting as much as I do, you'll wish I'd quit at the first line, so 'bye.

With much love to you & to the incomparable

Dartie—

Nelle

.   .   .

9

Adulation and Isolation

Life moved on from loss and inconvenience, for both Nelle and me. Our November visit to the Seattle Flynts, who then came to Alabama for the Christmas holidays, furnished a new cycle of little Harper stories to amuse her namesake. (In her reply, Nelle mistakenly refers to author P. G. Wodehouse as P. E. Waterhouse. But then, she may have meant the confusion as satire.)

The occasion of Nelle's birthday on April 28 always brought her a horde of visitors either in town already for the Alabama Writers Symposium or down just for the celebration. She made sure to remind me of her birthday each year because I had twice misremembered the date by a couple of days. I think her letter was a not-so-subtle reminder that she might not be the only one in her social circle with short-term memory problems.

In 2010 my friend John Shelton Reed, the noted southern writer and sociologist, then serving as chancellor of the prestigious and exclusive Fellowship of Southern Writers, asked me to inquire whether Nelle would accept election to the organization. I doubted it. Her physical problems restricted out-of-state travel; her 2008 trip to the White House to accept the Medal of Freedom had been an exception, with the journey even more arduous because she refused to fly and so had to take a train. In 2011 she declined to make the trip again when President Barack Obama awarded her the National Medal of the Arts. Although Bush had declared *Mockingbird* to be his favorite book, he'd apparently forgotten that in an earlier presidential interview he had reserved that distinction for the Bible. Obama had better standing, having been seen purchasing a copy of the novel for daughter Malia while the family vacationed on Martha's Vineyard.

To persuade Nelle to accept the invitation of the Fellowship of Southern Writers, the only strategy I could think of was to invoke the playwright and screenwriter Horton Foote, one of her dearest friends. He'd written the screenplay for *Mockingbird*, and his death, in March 2009, had deeply affected her. Pitching Nelle on the fellowship idea, I began by reciting a litany of famous southern writers and historians who'd been members:

Robert Penn Warren, Reynolds Price, William Styron, Ralph Ellison, Eudora Welty, Peter Taylor, Shelby Foote, Andrew Lytle, Cleanth Brooks, Wendell Berry, Ernest Gaines, C. Vann Woodward, John Hope Franklin, and, of course, Horton Foote. Nelle was unimpressed until I mentioned Foote, who for years before his death had begged her to accept election. On my second try, she finally consented, for Foote's sake, but stipulated two conditions: that she not be required to speak or attend, and that I accept for her and speak on her behalf.

And so, when the fellows and their fans assembled in Chattanooga, all hoping for a sighting of the literary icon, they got me instead. I talked, as much as I dared, about the Lee family and its most famous daughter, and why the fellows had made a wise choice in electing her.

I enclosed copies of my speech in letters to Nelle and Alice. When we brought the framed award to Monroeville, she added it to the eclectic collection of visuals already gracing the walls of her small apartment: photos of her with President and Mrs. Bush, a Steve Breen cartoon of an American eagle intensely reading *Mockingbird* on the fiftieth anniversary of its publication, a photo taken by Kathryn Windham of an African

American woman holding a rooster, and a commemorative block of stamps honoring Gregory Peck that we had once framed for her.

We delivered the award on a trip to attend her birthday celebration as well as the Alabama Writers' Symposium. Our reward was Nelle's good-natured grousing that we had neglected her in order to attend "a silly conference." That pretty much summarized her low regard for literary critics and their craft. (I sometimes wondered whether our friendship could have survived had my scholarly field been literature rather than history.) Dartie later sent Nelle a photo taken of the two of them during our visit.

In the middle of May Nelle mentioned in a letter that she'd begun to reread C. S. Lewis, an old favorite of hers and mine. What Dartie and I did not know at the time, but realized later, was that this was the last letter from Nelle we would ever receive.

◦ ◦ ◦

•   •   •

8 October '08

My dear Wayne:

You will, I trust, be my mouthpiece at the 6
November to-do [her induction into the Fellowship of
Southern Writers]. If I did not have you, I would perish.
I don't mean to sound ungrateful (yes I do), but I shall
never understand why people knowing my incapacity,
will bestow honors upon me & wish me to attend the
ceremonies. Oh, well!

Much love,
NELLE

•   •   •

18 October '08 [3 weeks after my mother's death]

My dear Wayne:

What a terrible time for you! At our age (or at least at
mine) we are no strangers to sadness, but it doesn't hurt
any less. Rather more, I think. Whoever said the older
you are, the better you are at "taking it" he (or she) was
wrong—it's the reverse.

MUCH LOVE,
NELLE

•   •   •

∘ ∘ ∘

January 6, 2009

Dear Nelle,

Well the firestorm named Harper has come and gone. I wish there were some way to eliminate the years from 2–5 from the chronology of childhood. She is prissy, whiney, won't eat normal food that others eat, and is generally a pain in the butt. And if that is the evaluation of her loving grandfather, you can imagine what others must think of her. The only redeeming fact is that she will be different tomorrow than she is today.

Dartie struggled through the holidays with a terrible chest cold, recovered, and has now relapsed into an even worse cold. She is off to the doctor tomorrow. Nonetheless, she enjoyed our delightful two grandsons, her sons, and a multitude of seldom-seen relatives.

I actually finished revising two chapters of my memoir [later published as Keeping the Faith: Ordinary People, Extraordinary Lives*] so I counted the holidays a success both in good cheer and productive writing. I also read Madison Jones' new novel* The Adventures of Douglas Bragg*. It is quite a change from all his other works—a blend of John Kennedy O'Toole's* Confederacy of Dunces *and the various light-hearted romps of Clyde Edgerton (*Raney*,* Walking Across Egypt*,* In Memory of Junior*). Very funny, but*

more a string of anecdotes than a substantive novel. I will
probably read a little history now and return to writing the
memoir.

I hope Miss Alice feels better now and that you have
escaped the dread miasma. Give her our regards.

Sincerely,

Wayne

o o o

25 January '09

My dear Both:

I should be strung up & flogged at the Masthead
for not having written you; I am afflicted with
ineluctable laziness—the days pass here with deadly
same-ness and I complain when I should be counting
my blessings, two of which are Wayne & Dartie. You
have brightened my life & every time you appear you
bring a silent message of joy (what is it? "Joy cometh
in the morning . . ."). I think it's from Ecclesiastes or
somewhere. I do know that it was a P. E. Waterhouse
title.

I love you.

N.H.

o o o

○ ○ ○

14 February '09

My dear Dartie,

Thank you for the picture of the world's most beautiful lady with the world's plainest!!

Hope you are enjoying the hours of solitude you must have with the Prof. writing his memoirs. Let's just hope they have the ring of truth even if they are fiction.

It's Hebrews 13:8 (King James) with a vengeance here—hope your life is filled with excitement!

Much love,
NELLE

○ ○ ○

。　。　。

1 March (??)

at any rate, it's Sunday

My dear Wayne:

    Is there some sort of function at which we should
be present on 28 April? It's not your birthday, wedding
anniversary or anything important. It is, however,
my birthday; otherwise I would not have the shred of
memory I have about something taking place.

    If you know, or ascertain please advise. With much
love from Dartie's co-conspirator!

。　。　。

March 10, 2009

Dear Nelle,

    *I enquired among your usual suspects, and one of them
(Cathy Randall by name) divulged that State Archivist Ed
Bridges is indeed planning some sort of birthday event for
you and all your pals. We plan to be there for sure if only to
amuse, entertain, and harass you lest you hear too many
superlatives and come to believe they are all true.*

    Meantime if you need some meat to feed your ego, I

have included a report on online computer visits to the
Encyclopedia of Alabama. We now average about 13,000
visits a week (a total of 600,000 page visits since we
launched in September). The #2 subject is some character
named Nelle Harper Lee and the #8 subject is the book
she wrote. I guess that makes you more popular than Bear
Bryant, George Wallace, Hank Williams and even Wayne
Flynt.

Love,
Wayne and Dartie

•   •   •

. . .

18 March '09

Dearest Wayne:

Please forgive this less than prompt reply, but MY PUBLIC keeps me so busy, I don't have time for friends.

You see in an instant that this is a lie. The truth is: the less I do, the lazier I get, and now I can hardly move. Something did, though, the other day—I stood straight up. The good fortune of my friend Kevin Howell brought me to my feet: he was an editor at the HarperC—lost his job a month ago. The spectacular news is that he's got a <u>new</u> job at Penguin Books! He was without work for only 1 month. He celebrated by sending me a yard's length of boxes of candy! Ya'll come share it!

MUCH LOVE, NELLE

. . .

• • •

Dear Nelle,

What great news about Kevin Howell. We thought so often of you when Horton Foote died, knowing of your long and loving friendship. We knew how upset you were. So the good news about Kevin is welcomed by all. Isn't it strange how bad news spreads from one person to that person's friends like a giant cloud of dark foreboding. And good news travels just as quickly as a fresh Spring breeze on a bright sunny day. Good news has a Robert Frost quality to it, bad news a Franz Kafka sense of despair.

I wish we could share your chocolate right now, but I am having some minor surgery Tuesday. So, we will try to haul Kathryn Windham down that way later in April. We will also see you on your birthday on April 26 at the Archives. I have been drafted to say a few words about our esteemed friend. If given the entire month to extol your virtues, I told them, I could do you justice. If given only 10 minutes, I am free to make up whatever I choose. No telling what kind of fiction this old historian may concoct.

We think of you often and pray for you unceasingly, as the Bible says. Say hello to Miss Alice for us.

Sincerely,
Dartie and Wayne

• • •

°   °   °

28 March '09

Beloved Prof:

Your letter was a beauty, for which much thanks!
One minor thing, though—if you extol my virtues on
26 April, you will be 2 days early. I think our meeting is
on the 28th, which <u>is</u> my birthday. At any rate, I'll take
praise whenever I can get it!

It's strictly Hebrews 13:8 here; a visit from you & my
co-conspirator would be most welcome if you are on the
way back from the flesh-pots of Biloxi or somewhere.

Much love,

NELLE

°   °   °

* * *

April 4, 2009

Dear Great Writer,

Well, if I can forget my wife's birthday, my grandchildren's birthday, and my own birthday, I don't see why I can't forget your birthday. Besides, I only missed by 2 days. Rather than spend April 26 and 27 in Montgomery, we will drive over on the 28th. Do you need any help blowing out all those candles? Dartie could get on one side, and I could blow from the other side, and we might make Montgomery a seaport!

Wayne & Dartie

* * *

April 14, 2009

Dear Nelle,

I celebrated income tax day eve by watching "Gone With the Wind" on Turner Movie Classics. I believe the book was written by one of those "one book" southern writers. Last time I checked, you were outselling her two to one. But then your South is a lot more convincing than hers was. And I like Scout lots better than Scarlett, though her (Scarlett's) amorality fits lots of southerners I know. Only a writer from

Atlanta could fully appreciate the crass materialism of the New South. As my sociologist friend John Shelton Reed has written, "Every time I go to Atlanta, I am reminded what 240,000 Confederate soldiers died to prevent."

I am writing you during the intermission. I hope the outcome will be better in the second half but fear that our gallant lads will lose again. Damn those venal Yankees! See you soon birthday girl!

Sincerely,
Wayne

· · ·

16 April '09

Dear Ones:

　　See ya in Montgomery on the 28th!

　　(That is, if I can see!)

　　It's strictly Hebrews 13:8 here, so, so long—

Much love,
NELLE

· · ·

●　●　●

19 April '09

Dearest Both:

Come on! There are no two people in this world I'd enjoy seeing as much as you!

Wayne, you & the incomparable Dartie mean so much to me, especially now that I'm old & afflicted. Your two merry selves are entities that mean good cheer, wisdom, & much laughter when you appear on the scene. Come soon! Stay long!

Much love,
NELLE

●　●　●

3 May (?)

My Both:

It was an unmitigated pleasure to be in your company. Only one thing the matter: your visit was far too short! You should have spent your every moment entertaining me instead of attending a silly conference.

Of course, nothing here on a steady basis, so I have nothing to report, except that I love you much.

NELLE

• • •

Dear Madam Famous Author,

Thanks for allowing us to intrude on your time between the clamoring throngs of visitors trying to have an audience with you. . . .

We seem to never get enough time for conversation, but we were afraid that three days in a row with us might exhaust your patience.

It was also wonderful to see Miss Alice if only for a short time.

We are off Monday to care for the little charmer [Harper Flynt in Seattle] with the silly grin on the other side. Mom and Dad are off to Italy for 10 days. If we survive, we will be down to see you in late May or early June.

Wayne

• • •

13 May '09

My dearest Both:

I am crazy, so I don't remember if it's Dartie or Wayne to whom I owe a letter: probably both of you— hence this salutation. My recent readings, if you are even faintly interested, have been centered on C. S.

Lewis: I have come back to him in my old age, after decades of neglect, and I am surprised to discover how much I've missed his wise and humorous counsel—he was a sweetheart! The latest two Lewis anecdotes I heard were delightful, but I have room for only one: he was asked if he remembered the instructions he received as a boy. "Only two," he said. "Bend over," and "Don't talk with your mouth full."

They don't make 'em like him any more. But there's you, my friend, Wayne!

Much love,

NELLE

●   ●   ●

10

To Everything a Season

Nelle's sister Louise died in October 2009 at age ninety-three, not only ending her own sad saga, but also dealing another bitter blow to a family reeling from illness and aging. I have written many letters of consolation, but the ones to Nelle and Alice were among the hardest. Since they were both too infirm to attend Louise's graveside service, I wrote to them about it. Louise had always wanted to hear "Amazing Grace" played on bagpipes at her funeral. That wasn't possible, but her great-granddaughter provided a wonderful alternative.

Although Nelle rarely went to Montgomery at this stage in her life, she did attend the fall induction ceremony of the Alabama Academy of Honor, where she could socialize with old friends.

We continued to write to Nelle and Alice and drive to Monroeville to see them. On one visit in 2011, I recommended they read Zora Neale Hurston's novel *Their*

Eyes Were Watching God. Alice ordered it, and the book triggered memories of family history and her own childhood. Although Nelle ceased her correspondence with us, Alice continued writing, and we saw that history fascinated her as thoroughly as fiction did Nelle. The two had lived very different lives. While Nelle enjoyed New York's Broadway shows and art galleries, Alice had spent her time wandering down back roads in Southwest Alabama with like-minded friends, rescuing letters and papers from deserted plantations, tenant shacks, or abandoned garages, scrutinizing old mills or country stores for records, and sharing local history stories with three generations of family and friends.

The Doy Leale McCall Collection that Alice describes resulted from lifelong efforts by a pioneer Southwest Alabama timber family to discover, buy, and preserve more than a million documents pertaining to the state—Civil War diaries, presidential land grants, descriptions of slave life, and much more—from territorial days into the early twentieth century. The family's 2011 gift to the University of South Alabama had an estimated value of $3.1 million and was considered at the time to be one of the most important archives of nineteenth-century history preserved by any southern state. Alice had known three generations of McCalls and was eager for me to explore the collection, housed in Mobile. As her letters meticulously recounted South Alabama and family history, I began to wonder if Alice's mind was not superior to the new million-document archive as a source of local history, and this only months shy of her hundredth birthday.

In June 2011 Nelle and Alice lost another connection to the past, Kathryn Windham, who, like Louise, died at age ninety-three. I sent Alice my newspaper column eulogizing Kathryn.

Alice's hundredth birthday on September 11, 2011, was, at her instruction, a small affair. I offered a brief tribute to her legal career and knowledge of history and gave her a copy of my memoir *Keeping the Faith*, which had been published weeks earlier and for which Nelle had written a blurb.

The last letter in this chapter also turned out to be my last letter to Nelle. It had been some time since she was able to respond, so although we would visit her in Monroeville again many times before her death, about a year later, I had to face the fact that our correspondence, so precious to me for so long, was over.

∘　∘　∘

• • •

October 21, 2009

Dear Nelle,

We enjoyed seeing you, both in Monroeville and Montgomery. We tried not to monopolize your time in the capitol, though it was hard. Hopefully we will see you in Eufaula this Sunday.

We both grieve over Louise's passing. She was a dear friend we loved long before we knew you. I will always remember her family stories about Finch's Landing, about the eccentrics in Eufaula, about a local Baptist preacher who apparently murdered not one wife, but two.

As you may know already, she was a real force for social justice in the town. At a critical moment, the mayor appointed her to a committee on public education designed to make integrated schools so successful all students would want to attend. Her reputation for dignity and integrity served the cause well.

Of course, I agree with your father that this parting is for a season only. We will one day have a great reunion punctuated, I hope, by a splendid bagpiper, playing "Amazing Grace." For the time being, we must settle for a fiddle version, which will be fine.

I once took a philosophy of religion course in order to study the problem of suffering. Predictably, we reached no answers better than Job's: "Though he slay me, yet will I trust him."

So, I turn instead to my favorite Appalachian novel, Charles Frazier's Cold Mountain, *for comfort. He puts these profound words in the mind of his goat woman/herb doctor: "That's just pain. It goes eventually. And when it's gone, there's no lasting memory, not the worst of it anyway. It fades. Our minds aren't made to hold on to the particulars of pain the way we do bliss. It's a gift God gives us, a sign of His care for us."*

Wayne

o   o   o

October 29, 2009

Dear Alice and Nelle,

The memorial service for Louise was wonderful. It was a bright, crisp day overlooking the Chattahoochee River, with some 75–100 of her friends and relatives present. Her sons, grandchildren, and great grandchildren were there. Although there was no bagpiper, I am sure Louise was quite content with her great granddaughter playing "Amazing Grace" on the fiddle. The little girl was wonderful: poised, smiling, intense, and very proud of herself. Louise, I am certain, was smiling all through the song.

Rev. Joe Lisenby, who eulogized her, knew her well and did her justice. He mentioned her concern for fairness and justice, her involvement in committees for improved race relations and better funded schools in Eufaula. He told stories about her that were both humorous and insightful. Dr. Al Harbour mentioned his relationship with you through the West Florida–South Alabama Methodist Conference and the Finch family. The liturgy was appropriate and simple, as she would prefer.

Afterwards, Gwin Conner invited us to join the family at her house to talk about Louise, Alice, Nelle, and family. That too would have delighted her. Ed and Hank told stories and shared memories.

Although you were missed, you did the better thing by spending lots of quality time having fun in better days. As for Louise, she has left the land of shadows for the realm of light, she now knows as she is known, and I rejoice for her liberation.

Sincerely,
Wayne and Dartie Flynt

o o o

°   °   °

11–11–09

Dear Wayne and Dartie:

Thank you for your lovely letters to Nelle Harper and me both before and after the memorial service for Louise. We were especially grateful to view the service through the eyes of a non-member of the family.

The little girl whom you describe as very proud of herself as she filled in the spot for the not available bagpiper was 11 year old Sara Byers, the great-granddaughter of Louise. Since she was five years old Sara has played violin with the Jacksonville Junior Symphony Orchestra, the youngest member ever to that date. She is being educated in the public schools of Jacksonville as a gifted child.

I do not have to tell you how proud we are of Sara and with what interest we watch her progress. It may amuse you to know that Sara is half-Scottish, her father being a native of Scotland but now a naturalized American citizen and an educator.

Nelle Harper and I have been recalling some of the great trips we made with Louise. We three sisters really enjoyed our own company. Once we heard that a friend described us as follows: "They laugh a lot; they enjoy their own company; they can't agree on a single thing, not even the temperature."

I hope your travels bring you in this direction soon. Your visits are like a shot of B-12 to Nelle.

God Bless,
Alice

     ·   ·   ·

March 2, 2011

Dr. J. Wayne Flynt
1224 Penny Lane
Auburn, AL. 36830

Dear Wayne,

I am about half-way through "Their Eyes Were Watching God," and I am enjoying it very much—no trouble with the dialect.

I had never heard of Zora Neale Hurston nor any of her writings. I could not see how that would happen. Then I saw 1937 was the year of its publication and realized that at the time I was making the move from Monroeville to Birmingham and the transition had cut my reading time for a period of time.

Reading this book caused me to look back into the

history of the family. Two of my great-great grandfathers came to Monroe County in its early years, one in 1823 and the other a few years later. Each of them became the owners of considerable acreage and common sense should tell me that they needed help to cultivate the cotton fields and to cut down trees for sawmilling. But I always thought my forbearers [sic] too poor to afford slaves. In recent years I have run across some old tax assessment sheets. One of them shows Dr. R. Maiben 39 slaves; for T. H. Williams a longer list of names but no total.

I have no idea of knowing what became of the people after 1863, but I strongly expect they took the surnames of their former owners and possibly actually never left. I am basing this on the fact that those names are prevalent among the black people living in that same area of Monroe County today. When I was a small child visiting my Grandmother Finch, I happily played with Fanny Lee Penn, my own age, and the only child in the neighborhood. She was named for my mother who was Frances Lee.

My Grandfather Finch actually owned a slave, but he probably never knew it. He was a young child living in Virginia. His Grandmother died in Alabama and under the terms of her will, each of her three grandchildren was to receive one slave. Minors could not under the law hold title to personal property and then came Emancipation.

One of my sitters, a tall black lady probably in her '70's has just told me rather proudly that her niece and three of her friends are now reading my book (Their Eyes Were Watching God).

It was great to visit with you and Dartie even though it was brief. Hope it won't be too long before your speaking engagements bring you this way again.

Devotedly,
Alice

o   o   o

April 19, 2011

Dear Nelle,

You are now officially inducted into the Fellowship of Southern Writers with all the privileges and rights pertaining thereto (there are NO privileges and rights except all those great writers were ecstatic to have the most famous of all Southern writers in their ranks). We met lots of people whose writing I enjoy: Josephine Humphreys, Wendell Berry, Natasha Trethewey, Bobbie Ann Mason, Ernest Gaines, Charles Frazier. Unfortunately, many of the best members are dead now: Eudora Welty, Flannery O'Connor, Reynolds Price, Horton Foote, Cleanth Brooks, Robert Penn Warren, Peter Taylor, Andrew Lytle.

*We will bring your award down on your birthday. We are
having it framed to add to all your presidential citations.*

Sincerely,
Wayne and Dartie

◦ ◦ ◦

5–1–11

Dear Wayne,

Thank you so much for the copy of your remarks on
the occasion of Nelle Harper's election to the Fellowship
of Southern Writers. You are most generous in your
assessment of the Lee Family as readers. If Louise were
with us, she would also express her appreciation. My
father read to me even after I learned to read, and he read
to his grandsons so they would become readers.

I cannot understand a person who doesn't read. That
person misses one of the greatest joys of life.

I hope your travels will return you and Dartie to
Monroeville soon. It's always a joy to visit with you.

God bless,
Alice

◦ ◦ ◦

◦ ◦ ◦

May 8, 2011

Dear Wayne,

Did you know about the McCall Collection that was
being presented to the University of Alabama as you
were visiting down on the meeting here? I knew of
the existence of the collection but knew nothing of its
financial value. Some expert said 1.3 million. Others say
it will make some changes in history.

If you are not familiar with the story of how it came to
be let me know and I'll write it to you.

You may make some changes in your summer plans
and find yourself in Mobile more than you intended.

Devotedly,

Alice

◦ ◦ ◦

. . .

May 10, 2011

Dear Alice,

I have read about the McCall Collection given to the University of South Alabama. The article I read summarized only a few items, all of which sounded fascinating. I presume it is heavily weighted toward the Gulf Coast, particularly Mobile. But given the importance of that city in antebellum Alabama, it will surely augment/ change many parts of state history. I would very much like to know the story of how it came to be, so write me when you can. We hope to come down next week. A film (documentary) about Mockingbird is being made, and the producer wants me to talk about the worldwide significance of the book (I am tempted to tell them about you instead). I am having the Gregory Peck plate block of stamps framed for Nelle and will bring them. We will also stop by to see you.

I have included this op. ed. from the Press-Register for you and Nelle.

Sincerely,
Wayne

. . .

•   •   •

June 27, 2011

Dear Miss Alice,

. . . I have enclosed some clippings about Kathryn Tucker Windham's memorial service. It was a wonderful celebration: funny; loving; joyful; touching. All that Kathryn was.

Rev. Donald Davis, her only peer as a story teller, was wonderful. He introduced the black carpenter who made her beautiful coffin of heart pine 20 years ago, and Charlie Lucas, who wrapped her body in a quilt made in Gee's Bend and lovingly laid it in the coffin.

Davis said that when Kathryn asked him to deliver the eulogy (because he was a Methodist, Southerner, and Democrat), she instructed him to keep it short: "People want to tell stories before and after the service. So just have your say and shut up." The spirit of Kathryn soared to heaven amidst Bluegrass music, stanzas of "I'll Fly Away," and much laughter.

Wayne

•   •   •

∘ ∘ ∘

7/9/11

The Chilton County peaches were great—the first that I have had this season. Shortly after you left my nephew came in, spied the blueberries and asked please don't eat them but save them until Marianne returns from visiting their new grandson. She would then make delicious blueberry muffins and all the family could enjoy them. Of course, I did as he requested.

It was great to have your visit, just not frequent enough. I can't wait to get a copy of your memoir. Until it is read, it will displace the four that I am reading.

Mother Nature has promised us a rain today, but thus far has not fulfilled that promise. We had a shower day before yesterday which broke the drought, but it was not nearly enough.

I had asked for no party on Sept. 11th. After having had 99, what is one more? But sometimes things like that get out of hand. Since that day is Sunday, perhaps not too many people will cut short worship services to get here.

Whatever the day, you are invited and I look forward to seeing you then.

Fondly,

Alice

● ● ●

July 12, 2011

Dear Alice,

I am glad you liked the peaches and blueberries. The peaches were ordinary but the blueberries have been superb this year. I am glad you could share them with family. I would have brought more had I known.

We thought Nelle was in unusually fine spirits Friday: Laughing; telling stories; animated.

Thanks for the invitation to your birthday. You already know my present, presumptuous as it is. I will bring you a copy of my memoir, so don't buy one.

We love you,
Wayne

● ● ●

December 1, 2011

Nelle: Nancy Anderson, an English professor at Auburn University in Montgomery, who (with Bert Hitchcock) wrote the wonderful essay about you for the on-line Encyclopedia of Alabama, asked me to give this information to you. She had an English student who has started a non profit press. The woman uses all the profits from the press to make books available to poor children in Alabama and Mississippi.

The woman's name is Ashley Gordon. She plans to publish an anthology of essays which have already been published in magazines or literary journals. She wants to include your essay entitled "Dear Opry." I told Nancy I would leave this with you and if you agree, I will give her your agent's contact information. But it is entirely up to you whether or not you want to fool with this since Nancy only asked me to inform you of it.

Dartie and I saw Geoffrey Sherman's musical production of Truman's <u>A Christmas Memory</u> last night at the Alabama Shakespeare Festival. I could not imagine how a musical could capture any of the wonderful sense of community and timelessness of small town life that Truman immortalized in his story. Amazingly, the music was consistent with the theme, though the girl who played a juvenile Nelle Harper was TERRIBLE. Obviously, no one has yet figured out what kind of 8 year old you were (a real hellion by our estimation). Conversely, both the boy who played the youthful Truman and the man who played the adult version (and narrator) were wonderful. The show was a fine launch of the holiday season for us. . . .

We will be along some time in the next several weeks to greet you and Miss Alice and to bring Dartie's appropriate

Christmas goodies offered on your behalf (no fruit cakes with whiskey, though; you know how much we dislike your depiction of Baptists, which is second only to your prejudice against Auburn fans)

> *Sincerely, your deeply humbled Auburn fans,*
> *Wayne & Dartie*

•   •   •

February 17, 2015

Dear Nelle (famous author of two <u>known</u> books & maybe more):

I told a reporter the story of "our" Seattle Harper, who when I called her a lady, quickly informed me that she was no lady; she was Harper Swann Flynt. She was 4 or 5 at the time. She is now 10. She went to a sleep-over at her best friend's house last week, and the little girl's mother said: "I understand you are no lady, Harper." Actually, she reminds both of us of you. Are you, or were you ever, a lady, Nelle? Actually our little demon is now the sweetest 10 year old charmer we know.

> *Wayne & Dartie*

•   •   •

• • •

March 1, 2015

Dear Nelle,

In the last USA Today Best-Selling Book List, TKAM has risen to #14 54 years, 7 months after publication.

I am also enclosing a promising report on treatment of macular degeneration from <u>The Economist</u>.

Finally, I also re-read Norman Maclean's novel, <u>A River Runs Through It</u>. At the end of the novella, Norman explains his dead brother, Paul, to their father: "you can love completely without complete understanding." Otherwise, I thought, only God could love us completely because only God understands us completely. Suddenly, after all these decades, I understood about Scout and Jem's relationship to Boo Radley and your relationship to Truman and Sook's relationship to Truman. Isn't it wonderful when bright light breaks through the heavy clouds of the soul.

We are bringing chocolate down to Monroeville on Sunday, March 8.

Love you,
Wayne & Dartie

• • •

Postscript

My last letter to Nelle was written a month after I, along with the rest of the world, heard the stunning news that a copy of her first manuscript had been found and would be published. The publisher's February 3 announcement of the book, which bore the cryptic title *Go Set a Watchman* (borrowed from Isaiah 21:6, King James Version, of course), spun her life into unfamiliar disorder. Evidence of what was to follow arrived two days later on February 5, when I spent nine hours talking with reporters calling from around the world.

Almost immediately questions arose about whether Nelle was too ill, physically and possibly mentally, to give informed consent to the publication of a book she had ignored for decades. In that frenzied climate, fueled by journalists as well as by Monroeville gossip, long-ago chatter about whether Truman Capote had really written *Mockingbird* was resurrected. Riding the crest of small-town resentment against Tonja Carter, the law partner Alice chose to carry on Nelle's legal business during the final years of her life, the rumors reached a worldwide audience. As the tsunami of rumors surged, my son, Sean, wrote me his fears about the possible effects of the controversy on Nelle: "They'll drag her out into the spotlight even if it kills her just so they can satisfy their curiosity. Reminds me of a 4th grade demonstration of a tortoise's beating heart. We saw it beat. The tortoise died."

Nelle's friends and family had noticed her growing problems with short-term memory but did not doubt her mental competence to give informed consent. Neither did officials from the elder abuse division of the Alabama Department of Human Resources, who investigated anonymous charges that Nelle was being mistreated. Not only did she pass whatever cognitive test they administered, she reportedly dismissed their intrusion into her private life by telling them to go to hell and leave her alone.

More particularly, Nelle's nephew Hank Conner, unofficial Lee family historian, confirmed her enthusiasm for publication of the manuscript, which he said he had read a half-century earlier and thought inferior to *Mockingbird*. During a two-day visit several weeks before the publisher's announcement, he said, he asked her multiple times if she was certain she wanted the novel to be published. Each time she replied that she did, finally satisfying the single person who understood the situation best and initially had been most skeptical.

During our first visit with Nelle on February 9, I was eager to administer my own memory test. As we tried to drive into the parking lot beside the assisted living facility, a vehicle from the state's Department of Human Resources blocked our way, and a guard checked our identification before granting us admission. Inside the building, the twelve residents, Nelle among them, cowered in the commons area, none of them joking or talking as they usually did. After we wheeled Nelle to her room, I jokingly called her the "great one" and mentioned her new novel. She shocked us by asking, "What new novel?"

"Don't talk like that, Nelle," I said. "I mean your new novel that has just been announced by HarperCollins."

"I don't have any new novel," she insisted. Now fully alarmed and wondering if the rumors of mental impairment could be true, I muttered, "*Go Set a Watchman*, Nelle. Your new novel."

"Oh," she replied with a grin. "That's not my new novel; that's my old novel."

I was filled with relief. "Well, whatever you call it, it just reached the top of the *New York Times* bestseller list."

"You lie!" she shouted, one of her favorite retorts when we bantered.

"I am an ordained Baptist minister. I don't lie," I responded.

She laughed. "Well, that makes it even worse."

"You should be so proud, Nelle," I said. "This is the most important story about American literature in half a century."

There was a long pause. With sagging shoulders and eyes focused on her feet, she muttered softly, almost inaudibly, "I'm not so sure anymore."

Publication on July 14 raised her spirits, as did our report during the day that the town was filled with reporters from around the world and, thanks to security at the Meadows, none of them could get near her. Early on the fifteenth we went by the Meadows to tell her that first-day sales had exceeded 700,000 copies, setting records for adult fiction at Barnes & Noble and Books-A-Million. Gleefully she replied, "I am a very rich woman!"

Dartie corrected her: "You have been a very rich woman for a very long time, Nelle!"

By the end of the first week, sales totaled more than 1.1 million, a record for an American novel.

Some critics declared Nelle's new/old novel a searing and accurate account of racism in the 1950s. Some saw it as a flawed work that nonetheless previewed the talent that later came to fruition in *Mockingbird*. Others dismissed the novel as unfinished, preachy, too long on dialogue and too short on wordsmithing and characterization. Many liberal northern readers were appalled at Jean Louise Finch's reconciliation with her racist father and uncle. Many conservative southern readers were appalled that Nelle had opened old wounds better left alone.

The controversy *Watchman* provoked set me to thinking about our quarter-century friendship with the three Lee sisters. I reread Nelle's classic novel as well as her new one, and found in them what I had first discovered in the Bible: the most elemental meaning of innocence, judgment, justice, mercy, love, tolerance, forgiveness, and reconciliation, between races as well as generations. I also reread one of Nelle's favorite novellas, Norman Maclean's *A River Runs Through It*, based on the biblical parable of the prodigal son. The upright brother tells his minister father the sparse details of the murder of his younger, dissolute brother Paul. His father replies, "Are you sure you have told me everything you know about his death?"

"Everything," Norman replies.

"It's not much, is it?" his distraught father asks.

"No," replies Norman, "but you can love completely without complete understanding."

That sentence could have served as Nelle's requiem, her last gift to her readers. They would have to love her without fully understanding her, for she would not be pulled into the spotlight for the sake of our curiosity.

In the early morning hours of February 19, 2016, seven months after the publication of *Watchman* and barely two months before her ninetieth birthday, Nelle Harper Lee died peacefully in her sleep at the Meadows. The following day I delivered as Nelle's eulogy "Atticus's Vision of Ourselves," the tribute I had written years earlier for the Birmingham Pledge Foundation's gala awards ceremony. So satisfied had she been with my interpretation of Atticus and her own literary legacy of racial tolerance and understanding that she insisted I change not a single line. I complied though with one addition: a sentence to demystify her hero as required by her own depiction of his flaws in *Go Set A Watchman*. As for a discussion of the private life of the author or her father, that would have to wait for another time. Nelle was buried in the small cemetery adjacent to the Monroeville United Methodist Church next to her father, mother, brother, and sister. At last she found rest and peace.

Appendix:
Eulogy for Nelle Harper Lee

"Atticus's Vision of Ourselves"

Birmingham Pledge Foundation Lifetime Service
Award to Harper Lee, 9/13/06

And Eulogy Delivered at the Funeral of
Nelle Harper Lee, 2/20/16

We gather tonight to honor a person, a writer, her father, her family, and her novel. That is a bit more than
I can manage in fifteen minutes, so I will stick with the
novel. But it might help us all to remember that we are
honoring both a person and a writer, and they are different. Persons have a right to be persons separate from
being writers.

Every book, be it fiction or nonfiction, is the projec-
tion of the writer's vision and values, so in some sense
we cannot separate them. A work of fiction might seem

an exception to this generalization, but I don't think so. As writer/storyteller Garrison Keillor once said, "Fifteen minutes after an accident, no two people can agree on the details of what happened. If it were not for the truth of fiction, there wouldn't be any truth at all."

So what truth have people around the world teased out of the pages of *To Kill a Mockingbird*?

Racial justice. Tom Robinson is a symbol of three centuries of apartheid and injustice toward Africans and African Americans. Don't expect me to accomplish in a few minutes what ethicists, philosophers, sociologists, psychologists, theologians, and historians have not been able to do in the past three centuries: untie the complex knot of racism in the world. Harper Lee could not figure it out. Nor could Atticus Finch, who asks in the novel: "Why reasonable people go stark raving mad when anything involving a Negro comes up, is something I don't pretend to understand." But there is a difference between Atticus and many of us. The inability to explain is not an excuse for spiritual amnesia. Just after his troubled query about racism, Atticus adds: "I just hope that Jem and Scout come to me for their answers instead of listening to the town." Beyond our embedded love for our communities, Lee seems to be saying, is our obligation to follow our own internal ethical compass. "The one thing that doesn't abide by majority rule," Atticus explains, "is a person's conscience." And that is precisely why Atticus Finch emerges as such a profoundly important figure in American literature. If the jurors represent us at our cautious, timid, fearful worst, Atticus is humanity at its best. And that is one reason the novel endures. In an age of antiheroes—political and corporate corruption, excesses of all kinds by celebrities and athletes; a world populated by Madonna, Paris Hilton, Abramoff, Scanlon—Americans have lost their pool of real-life heroes. So they seek them now in literature. And in Atticus Finch, they have found their favorite hero, the person more than any other they aspire to be like and they want to represent them at their best. Miss Maudie tries to explain all this to Jem: "I simply want to tell you that there are some men in this world who were born to do unpleasant jobs for us. Your father's one of them."

●　　●　　●

Class. Although the year that the book was published, 1960, ushered in a new and violent age of civil rights upheaval in America and primed the reading public to understand the work as a race novel, I believe it is just as much about class. Lee describes two poor white families, the poor but proud Cunninghams and the poor but not proud Ewells. The Cunninghams are the deserving poor whom we can and should help. Scout explains the difference by telling her first-grade teacher about her friend, young Walter Cunningham: "The Cunninghams never took anything off anybody, they get along on what they have. They don't have much, but they get along on it." Not everyone in her family has Scout's insight or her compassion. Her aunt Alexandra thinks differently, in conjunction with the traditional social and class distinctions so deeply rooted in America: "The thing is [Scout] you can scrub Walter Cunningham until he shines, you can put him in shoes and a new suit, but he'll never be like Jem. Besides, there's a drinking streak in that family a mile wide. Finch women aren't interested in that sort of people."

Then there are the "white trailer trash" Ewells. They are the historic undeserving poor, regarded with disdain and contempt even by Maycomb's blacks. They are the legendary "po' white trash" who fill Erskine Caldwell's novels, not just economically indigent but also morally degenerate. In Act I of the play, Miss Maudie tells the audience: "Everyone in Maycomb knows what kind of people the Ewells are." That line is always comforting to the audience because now it means they can sit back, relax, and enjoy the play. It is not about them. It is about the Ewells, all those undesirables who joined the KKK and lynch mobs. Trouble is, that is not the way Lee sees the matter. Bob Ewell is no more her chief villain, the moral cripple in the story, than are the twelve men good and true who make up the jury. They could have acquitted Tom Robinson had they chosen to weigh the evidence instead of succumbing to Maycomb's racial taboos. Though at the end of the play some audiences actually boo Robert E. Lee Ewell when he takes his bow onstage, the novel demands that we look for the villain inside ourselves. Ultimately it is all the good people of Maycomb who are silent in the face of injustice who murder Tom Robinson.

◦　◦　◦

Differences. One of the most important themes of the novel for our time is tolerance of people unlike ourselves. Boo Radley may be a subtheme to some, but not to homosexuals, who often see themselves in the character, locked behind four walls by people who fear anyone who is different. Not to private people who are constantly being psychoanalyzed by Type A personalities: Are they afraid of people? Are they afraid of failure? Are they painfully shy? Are they mentally deficient? Do they have dark secrets? Are they Muslims? Jews? Pentecostals? Evolutionists? In some places, perhaps even fundamentalist Baptists? Of all people who are different for any reason, Atticus reminds his children: "You never understand a person until you consider things from his point of view . . . until you climb into his skin and walk around in it."

Community. At the beginning of the novel, Jem and Scout debate when the story began. Jem insists it began when their new friend Dill came into their lives and excited curiosity about Boo Radley. Scout disagrees, believing the story began when their ancestors chose to settle in Maycomb County, Alabama. Maycomb is a specific name but not a specific place. In fact many readers of the book insist it is a story about their town and the people who live in it. They can and do give the characters the names of local people. Having lived in Sheffield, Gadsden, Anniston, and Dothan while growing up, I can tell you the novel could have been set in any of those places. As in Maycomb, every day lasted twenty-four hours but seemed much longer. But each one of those days was filled with exceptional people and extraordinary events that turn all of us Scouts into Jean Louises when we grow up. The point is that what happened in Maycomb could have happened in Fort Payne, Albertville, Demopolis, Brewton, Fairhope, and all the places in between. What happened in Maycomb did happen everywhere. To Jews in Prague; to homosexuals in Berlin; to Gypsies in Romania, Pentecostals in Russia, Muslims in Serbia. And it happened to Okies and Arkies in California's Imperial Valley in the 1930s, to Appalachian whites in Detroit in the 1940s, and to people from Birmingham moving to New York City and Los Angeles in the 1960s. It happened to all people everywhere who talk funny, look strange, have a different color skin, worship God differently or not at all, people who stay in houses and refuse to come out and conform to our expectations or allow us to stare at them. It happens to the different, the strange, the other. That is the reason the novel still sells nearly a million copies a year nearly half a century after publication: because it continues to ring true to human experience. That is why it is required reading in so many Irish, British, Canadian, Australian, New Zealand, Austrian, Dutch, Czech, and German schools, why it has been translated into some forty languages: because the story is a story of the human experience, not just the story of what happened in Maycomb, Alabama.

The endurance of *To Kill a Mockingbird* resides also in the intense half-century debate we have had in American education about moral values. Should public schools teach values? If so, what values? Whose values? Actually hundreds of thousands of American teachers resolved that debate long ago. They decided to teach Harper Lee's values. Or is it Atticus Finch's values? At any rate, they teach the moral values embedded in *To Kill a Mockingbird*. And at our best, I like to think they teach our values, core Judeo-Christian, American democratic values: tolerance, kindness, civility, charity, justice, the courage to face down a community or a family when they are wrong and the compassion to love them despite their flaws. Incidentally, I am not telling you anything you don't know already. How do I know that? Because there was a survey of English teachers in 1989 to determine what fiction they most frequently assigned to their students. In Catholic schools *To Kill a Mockingbird* was the fourth most frequently assigned book. In public schools the novel ranked fifth, in private schools, seventh. An estimated three out of four American high school students read the novel, ranking Lee behind only William Shakespeare, Nathaniel Hawthorne, and Mark Twain. A 1991 Library of Congress survey of 5,000 patrons asked them what book had made the biggest difference in their lives. They listed *To Kill a Mockingbird* second only to the Bible. In 1991 American librarians voted the book the best novel of the twentieth century. The American Film Institute rated the film version of the novel as the thirty-fourth best film ever made; and in 2003 they chose Atticus Finch as the greatest hero of American cinema. Greater than James Bond. Greater than Indiana Jones. Greater than Moses. Greater even than Superman himself. In 1999 *TV Guide* rated the movie fifth among its top fifty films. The Library of Congress also claims that the novel is the most popular selection for citywide literature programs that ask residents to read a common novel during a year as the basis for a conversation about community values.

In one of those fine moments of irony for which Alabama is renowned, a novel written by a woman from Monroeville on the edge of the state's infamous Black Belt has become the primary literary instrument worldwide for teaching values of racial justice and tolerance for people different from ourselves, and the necessity of moral courage in the face of community prejudice and ostracism. Don't you just love it?

Wayne Flynt, distinguished university professor,
Auburn University

Acknowledgments

——

This is the story of two extended Alabama families, containing too many names to list. Down in this part of America, family counts for a lot. We often protect each other's secrets at the expense of the stories we want to tell. And few families had more secrets than the Lee family of Monroe County, Alabama. Therefore, I owe the greatest debt of gratitude to three incredible Lee sisters—Alice "Bear" Lee; Louise "Weezie" Lee Conner; and Nelle Harper Lee, who became "Dody" to close family—because they trusted me with their stories, and believed me when I promised never to write about Nelle during her lifetime.

Louise's two gifted sons—Edwin Conner, retired professor of English at Kentucky State University; and Hershel "Hank" Conner, retired professor of communications at the University of Florida—contributed stories, family insights, and perceptive literary judgments.

Acknowledgments

Sara Ann Curry—widow of Edwin Lee, the Lee sisters' only male sibling, who died young—enlightened me about the family from the unique perspective of an in-law, though a treasured one.

Whereas I tend to be extroverted and talk more than listen, Dartie, my beloved wife of fifty-five years, is quiet, thoughtful, and, as a high school English teacher, attentive to language, accent, content, and idiom. Therefore she was an excellent source for what really happened during hundreds of conversations with the three sisters over more than three decades. And she was my most severe literary critic, always able and willing to say what she believed. I think Nelle was drawn to her more than to me at first.

As Alice and Nelle came to know our two sons, David and Sean, they liked them as well. The boys were authors in their own right and enjoyed a chance to critique my manuscript, heaping out deserved criticism and revisions. Our sons married Alabama sisters, Shannon and Kelly Rogers. Kelly earned a master's in public history at Wake Forest University, offering as her thesis a meticulous annotated transcription of her Civil War–era great-grandfather's letters to his wife, the perfect preparation for the tedious work of deciphering Alice's handwriting. Shannon edited as well.

Amid swirling Monroeville controversies concerning the health of Nelle and Alice, the provenance of the newly discovered *Go Set a Watchman* manuscript, and the role of Alice's personally selected law partner and successor, Tonja Carter, I tried to remain objective and independent. Although I barely knew Tonja when the controversies began in February 2015, she was from that day forward Nelle's fiercest protector, the family's most assiduous representative, and the international press's preferred villain. Still, it was Tonja who gave me the permission to reproduce these letters, allowing Nelle to speak for herself from beyond the grave. For that, I am very grateful.

Finally, thanks to Andrew Nurnberg, Nelle's agent and mine, for guiding me splendidly through the minefield of commercial publishing. He and Jonathan Burnham, senior vice president at HarperCollins, were enthusiastic about this project from the beginning. And Sara Nelson, my skillful editor there, though new to the company as I am, was clearly not new to the profession. With deadlines looming when she arrived and a hapless

Acknowledgments

Luddite author who hated technology as much as Nelle did, Sara guided me to a secure landing right on time. It not only takes a village to raise a child, it also takes both personal and corporate families to produce a book. This one is the proof.

About the Author

Dr. Wayne Flynt, professor emeritus in the department of history at Auburn University, is the author of thirteen books, and one of the most recognized and honored scholars of Southern history, politics, and religion. He has won numerous teaching awards and has been a distinguished university professor for many years. He lives in Alabama.